To the Gate of Hell

To the Gate of Hell

The Memoir of a Panzer Crewman

Armin Böttger

Translated by Geoffrey Brooks
Foreword by Charles Messenger

Frontline Books, London

First published in German in 2006 as *Im Panzer – Ich kam durch: Stationen und Impressionen des Lebenswges eines Panzersoldaten der deutschen Wehrmacht*

This English edition first published in 2012 by Frontline Books

an imprint of
Pen & Sword Books Ltd.,
47 Church Street, Barnsley, S. Yorkshire, S70 2AS.

Visit us at www.frontline-books.com, email info@frontline-books.com or write to us at the above address.

Copyright © Verlagshaus Würzburg GmbH & Co. KG,
Fleschsig Verlag, Beethovenstrasse 5B,
D-97080 Würzburg, Germany, 2006
Translation copyright © Geoffrey Brooks, 2012
Foreword copyright © Charles Messenger, 2012

ISBN 978-1-84832-643-9

CIP data records for this title are available from the British Library.

Printed and Bound by the MPG Books Group Ltd., UK

Typeset in 11pt Palatino by Mac Style, Beverley

Contents

Foreword

A rnim Böttger has produced a fascinating account built around his experiences as a Panzer crewman during the Second World War. It is supported by a wide array of photographs, taken with his own camera, which was clearly his most precious possession during the war. The style in which he writes is an intimate one; it is as though one is sitting over a glass of beer with him in a *Gasthaus*. This explains why, to an extent, the story he tells does meander and is not in strict chronological order.

In many ways he was typical of the generation which grew up under Hitler's thrall. Once his Freiburg school was saddled with a Nazi headmaster he had no option but to join the *Jungvolk* and then the Hitler Youth, although he felt uncomfortable in both of them. An intelligent boy, but with some weaknesses in his academic subjects, he decided to volunteer for the Army before he was conscripted. In this way he could be granted his *Abitur*, the school leaving certificate which opened the door to a university education, without sitting the exams for it. Originally trained as a tank driver, he decided that being a radio operator was preferable. He spent considerable time at a Panzer depot at Sagan in Lower Silesia, which was where Stalag Luft III of "Great Escape" fame was also situated. It was on account of medical problems that Böttger remained there for so long, but he was involved in delivering new tanks to Italy, for onward transfer to North Africa, and Russia.

Not until April 1943, after two years at Sagan, was the author finally posted to a combat unit. This was the 24th Panzer Regiment of 24th Panzer Division, which was refitting in France after being virtually destroyed in the debacle of Stalingrad. The division had originally been the 1st Cavalry Division and its members kept the cavalry tradition alive through the use of cavalry ranks and calling their sub-units squadrons instead of companies. The reconstituted division was initially trained on self-propelled assault guns, but did eventually receive Panzer IVs. It was then deployed to northern Italy in the aftermath of Mussolini's fall, but saw no action there, since the Eastern Front beckoned once more.

With the failure of Operation Citadel in July 1943 the German Army in Russia was now firmly on the defensive. Böttger saw his first combat in the defensive fighting on the River Dnieper at the end of October and thereafter in the Nikopol bridgehead. His next experience of action was in Romania during early summer 1944. The division was then transferred to Poland and it was during the tail end of the major Soviet Bagration offensive that his tank was hit and he was badly burned.

After time in hospital, Böttger was posted to Zinten in East Prussia and became a courier. As such, he witnessed the remorseless Russian advance through East Prussia. With Army Group North becoming trapped, he was forced to escape across the ice of the Frisches Hoff, with thousands of refugees, and eventually reached Danzig, where he was put in a train and finally ended up at Erfurt. Here he heard that his old division was in Prague and used his own initiative to rejoin what remained of it. By now the end of the war was nigh and it became a question of attempting to surrender to the Americans rather than the Russians. This he was able to do and eventually managed to get back to his home town of Freiburg and begin rebuilding his life.

Arnim Böttger never regarded himself as a professional soldier and saw the war as a major disruption to his life, leaving him with no control over it. There was much about the Army which he disliked, yet he did feel intense loyalty to his comrades in 24th Panzer Regiment, especially 12 Squadron. He also did take pride in being awarded the Iron Class II and, more particularly, the Panzer Combat Badge. He learnt to adopt the tricks of the "old soldier", not least the principle of never volunteering for anything. Indeed, this helped him from avoiding being sent back to the front as cannon fodder during the last desperate months of the war. He portrays well how the combat soldier's life boiled down to very basic desires – food, drink, leave, mail, and girls, but not necessarily in that order. He also gives some touching sketches of some of those he served with, both the men he admired and others he hated.

Apart from his obvious loathing of the Nazi regime, one aspect which arouses his ire is that of atrocities. The publication of Omer Bartov's *The Eastern Front 1941–1945: German Troops and the Barbarisation of Warfare* in 1986 caused a stir because it argued that atrocities were not merely the province of the Waffen-SS, but were endemic in the German Army. At much the same time an exhibition was staged in the Federal Republic entitled *War and Annihilation – Crimes of the Wehrmacht 1941–1945*. The impression that both gave was that the German wartime generation was an evil one and made the likes of Böttger feel that they were becoming outcasts in their own country in much the same way that many US soldiers felt returning home after fighting in Vietnam. He himself blames this attitude on Left Wing elements in Germany and makes the point that such was the nature of the Hitler regime the average German was powerless to do anything about the excesses that were being committed. As it was, he witnessed no atrocities himself and never heard of any. Likewise, while he was well aware of the concentration camps, he had no idea of the Holocaust.

This is a very revealing book, looking as it does at the German Army of the Second World War from the viewpoint of the lower ranks. It provides insights on how and why the German soldier continued to fight on when clearly the war could no longer be won. It is a very personal story and one feels Arnim Böttger's hopes and fears throughout. His numerous photographs enhance what he writes and help to make the book a unique record.

Charles Messenger, 2012

Translator's Note

Where a person is identified by name and rank in the text, I have left the rank untranslated. Whereas in British military practice the only rank below that of an NCO is "Private" or "Trooper" etc. depending on the branch, in Germany Army usage there were four levels equivalent to a private soldier: *Schütze* (rifleman, an untrained recruit): *Oberschütze* (rifleman out of basic training): *Gefreiter* (Private Soldier) and *Obergefreiter* (Private Soldier, senior grade usually after two years' service). Whereas the holder of the latter rank could be given occasional power and duties which might resemble those of a British lance-corporal, the *Obergefreiter* was not an NCO. The highest rank attained by Adolf Hitler attained in his service in the First World War was *Obergefreiter* and thus contrary to the historical tradition he was never a corporal. That is why it is considered extraordinary that he should have had the Iron Cross, First Class while being a non-NCO (J. C. Fest).

The German Army had no lance-corporal rank. The lowest ranking NCO was an *Unteroffizier* (full corporal). It should be noted that *Unteroffizier* is also the generic term for "NCO" in German, i.e. any rank from corporal to WO I. In the Panzer Arm, the ascending ranks were the old Cavalry ranks of *Wachtmeister* (sergeant), *Oberwachtmeister* (master sergeant) and up to *Hauptwachtmeister* (WO I). The latter rank would be held by the company or squadron sergeant-major and the holder was always known as the *Spiess*, this term being retained in the book wherever the author uses it.

Panzer officers' ranks are less problematical: *Leutnant* (second lieutenant): *Oberleutnant* (first lieutenant): *Hauptmann* or *Rittmeister* (captain): *Major*: *Oberstleutnant* (Lt-Colonel): *Oberst* (Colonel) and so on.

In the German educational system the *Abitur* was and is the school-leaving certificate essential for university entry, and the *Abiturient* is a pupil studying for it. These two terms I have left untranslated where they occur.

Author's Introduction

"Who talks of victories? Survival is everything."

Rainer Maria Rilke

In the period between 1933 and the end of the Second World War I took countless photographs, beginning in the Hitler-Jugend and the majority later in the Wehrmacht. Many of these photos, some taken under the most difficult conditions, accompany the text and reflect not only my own personal experience, but the typical experience of a young man drawn into the war on the side of Hitler's Germany.

My passion for photography grew during the war once I decided on the idea of recording life in a panzer regiment. My desire to keep taking photos as if I were a war correspondent led me to do so during engagements and, if the circumstances allowed, during the heaviest fighting. So important was my camera to me that I kept it attached to the cord from which I was supposed to hang my service pistol around my neck, as was the panzer custom. Thus the day came when my panzer was hit and burst into flames, and I baled out wounded and unarmed on to the battlefield.

I used to send the rolls of film to my mother, who would then have them developed and returned to me at the front. For the present book I had a collection of over 500 monochrome and 150 colour prints to choose from. I took these with a simple Kodak Retina 1 without distance meter or light gauge and using Agfa film. They complete my story, and enable me to ensure that nothing has slipped my memory.

The many letters I wrote to my mother serve as a diary, depicting events exactly as they occurred and coincide chronologically with the photos. The photographs and letters, all previously unpublished, lay forgotten for years in a drawer before the idea possessed me to use them in an authentic real-time account of my personal experience. From that this book eventually evolved.

The first edition of my book was entitled *Durchkommen war alles* – "Survival was Everything". In it I described the life of a young German of those times – always in uniform, whether of the *Jungvolk*, Hitler-Jugend, the compulsory work service RAD and the Wehrmacht – and taught to obey all orders unconditionally. The material for the new edition was subjected to unsparing review. After the war ended we faced the question "What now?" This was answered in the subsequent edition when I set about using the opportunities which a life lived in freedom and without compulsion offers in the sense of Nietzsche: "Wie ich wurde was ich bin" (How I became what I am.)

The book elucidates the career of the anonymous panzer man. He had no right to an opinion, his life was governed by orders and ever-present anxiety. He had to obey, take part in panzer battles and witness the death of comrades at first hand. That was the German soldiers' lot.

Armin Böttger

Chapter 1

The Reich Work Service (RAD)

Following the conclusion of the French campaign in the summer of 1940, victorious German troops returned through my home town Freiburg im Breisgau. The end of this particular war unleashed in our people tremendous jubilation, and many of the young men standing on the pavements were already full of the yearning to fight, soldiers in spirit. People waved, pressed flowers into the hands of soldiers or applauded the marching ranks of troops from the windows of houses adorned with swastika flags. As an observer of this scene even I could not hold back a certain feeling of enthusiasm. I remember the radio broadcasting a special bulletin that Luftwaffe fighter pilot Werner Mölders had shot down his fortieth enemy aircraft. Joyfully, I went at once to pass the information to my mother. She would hear nothing about such details and told me crossly, "What of it, it will only lengthen the war." From the day of its outbreak my mother was convinced that this war could not be won!

By then my father was already deceased. Before the First World War he had been a corporal of the reserve in the Saxon horse artillery as a result of which he had a certain weak spot for the military. During the Great War as director of the Lörrach-UK gasworks he had a reserved occupation and so had not been called up. Once he drove to the front lines in his car and brought back a photograph of a British tank. In 1908 he had become a freemason, but even in the Hitler period he retained his love for uniforms and the military. His death early in 1938 spared him persecution in the conflict between freemasonry and the National Socialist State.

As regards myself, his son, his early death also spared him the disappointment that, despite my having obtained the *Abitur* school-leaving certificate, after four and a half years in the Wehrmacht I would return home not as a highly decorated officer but only a corporal. In time he might have come to think it better to have a son home from the wars as a mere infantryman rather than a heroic dead officer.

My decision to volunteer for the Wehrmacht had very little to do with this thinking. I admit that I was enthusiastic at the quick victories over Poland and France, but my real reason for volunteering was my school grades. Though tolerably good, some difficulties could be foreseen when the Abitur examinations came round. A pupil in his final year at school who volunteered for the Wehrmacht was awarded the *Abitur* without sitting an examination, and as a 17-year-old I took advantage of the opportunity. Thus I entered the Wehrmacht a few months earlier than my classmates, but arrived at the front much later than they did because of a long period I spent with a reserve unit.

On 1 October 1940 I put on the brown uniform of the Reich Work Service (RAD). The camp (K1/296) was situated on the edge of a forest just outside the little village of Wutzelhofen near Regensburg which for those current circumstances was very far from home. Here I experienced the first hard drill. The RAD leaders who would take charge of my life over the next two months were on the whole uncouth, often stupid and acted accordingly. When asked by a Feldmeister (lieutenant) for my calling or trade I told him, "Studying for my *Abitur*", to which he replied, "I'll put down 'None' then". Pointing out that "studying for one's *Abitur*" was not an occupation was technically correct, but was intended to express his prejudice against a social class. He had to make it clear more than just in principle who was the real master here.

The RAD leaders were one's superiors in a meaningless third-rate National Socialist organisation which was not taken seriously, at least not by the Wehrmacht. Later in training as a Wehrmacht recruit there was another reaction to the claimed occupation of *Abiturient*. These people were not happy with the answer 'nothing' and ordered the student to actually write "I am nothing". All this was part and parcel of a system whose purpose was to denigrate us morally and educate us to be soldiers without a will of our own.

After basic training, in which a spade replaced the usual rifle for our military-type exercises, came the real RAD activity, working as lumberjacks in the woodlands of the Prince of Thurn und Taxis. This involved felling trees, sawing the trunks, cutting away the branches and peeling off the bark, then stacking and loading the logs. We were quick to appreciate that as opposed to chopping down trees, the easy job was stripping the bark and lopping off branches. Each morning the various tools would be piled up waiting for our troop. At the word of command we had to sprint to these tools and grab one. The tool one chose determined one's activity for the day and how one would feel at the end of it.

In my group was a friend of mine from Freiburg. We would run together to the pile, our common intent being to obtain a pair of the same tools suitable for the lighter work. We were nearly always successful in this aim, but even so, these simple jobs were heavy going for us 17-year-olds. We were kept at this forced labour for weeks. I had volunteered for the Wehrmacht, but not for forced labour with the RAD. After six weeks the troop was relocated to the vicinity of Cham to build barracks for the female RAD. It was there that I received my call-up for the Wehrmacht.

Chapter 2

A Recruit Twice Over

"Whoever is not ill-treated cannot be trained."

Goethe

Upon induction into the Wehrmacht in December 1940, I went first to the training depot at Donaueschingen, about sixty kilometres from my home town of Freiburg. On the extensive terrain I began my training as a recruit with 14.Panzerjäger Inf.Komp.503, an infantry anti-tank company.

Entering the Wehrmacht, every soldier received identity discs which were to last him throughout his service. They could not be exchanged or altered and had to be worn around the neck permanently. They were of an oval shape with a centre line split in three places to make them easy to snap apart in case of death, when half would be left with the body and the other half used for administrative purposes. The bearer's blood-group was engraved on the discs. In my case an error had been made in determining my blood as group B, and this was on the tags. I did not know it then but my blood is AB and therefore I was lucky not to need a blood transfusion when the time came since it would have provoked a haematologic crisis.

Basic training included learning how to stand to attention, march and salute. Special instruction was given in the small 3.7-cm anti-tank gun. The majority of recruits were men out of their teens who had been following a trade such as builder, wine-grower on the Kaiserstuhl [a low mountain range in the south-west of Baden-Württemberg] or artisan: there were also a few school-leavers such as I.

The main result of our basic training was that we learned to shirk. A recruit would be posted in a favourable position in the vehicle hall to watch out for an officer. While we had the all-clear we sat or stood around our gun and did practically nothing. If an officer appeared there would be a sudden flurry of activity with the gun. Because the officers only rarely checked to see what we were doing, we had it really easy in our recruit training.

I spent my first war Christmas at Donaueschingen. I spent the next four Christmases far from home. This first Christmas I received a gift parcel from the Black Forest Union. It contained a Reclam paperback containing a commentary on Grimmelshausen's *Zum silbernen Stern* by H. E. Busse, a pocket calendar and a handsome pencil made from German silver with the inscription "War Christmas 1940 – Black Forest Union." The Freiburg tennis club also favoured its junior member with a Christmas parcel. From then on my home province had to look to itself much more and no further parcels were ever received.

Despite the comfortable life with the infantry, one day I volunteered for the panzers. It was the second time I had volunteered, and again it was to obtain an advantage for myself. I thought: "The infantry does a lot of running in open terrain and get wet when it rains." Since Donaueschingen had a particularly cold winter that year it was not difficult for me to imagine the lot of the infantryman when it froze. "In a panzer you have protection against the elements and above all no marching, and after a fight you pull out of the frontline in your panzer to a protected position in the rear."

Later, after being a panzer man for some time, I was asked on several occasions if I wanted to transfer to the SS panzers. What would have awaited me in the Waffen-SS? The exchange of information amongst the men in the various branches of the land forces was on the whole very good throughout the war. One heard useful things from this or that soldier while out on the town, on leave, or during a train journey. So I knew that the SS had better armaments. From the middle of the war the SS divisions were equipped mainly with Panther or Tiger panzers. In contrast to the Mark IV, the principal Wehrmacht panzer, they had a better gun, which could be a decisive factor during a panzer attack in determining whether you or the enemy sustained a mortal hit. They were also better armoured, and thus had more protection. As my colleagues and I discovered when we visited an SS unit in Russia, their clothing was better; for example, in the winter in Russia with the Wehrmacht I had no fur boots because my shoe size was out of stock. This could never have happened in the Waffen-SS. Their provisions were better too. My decision not to transfer over was based ultimately on my seeing the Waffen-SS as an extension of the *Jungvolk* and Hitler Youth for grown-ups. I did not want political pressure. That being said, we saw the Waffen-SS merely as soldiers like ourselves.

After volunteering for the panzers, on 1 January 1941 I reported to Panzer Abteilung (Battalion) 7 at Böblingen. Now I was a recruit for the second time, and it was not at all like it had been before. I was dreadfully depressed, and after a few days wrote to my mother, telling her how I longed for the quiet life at Donaueschingen. As a recruit "on the grindstone" I even saw how mild school had been, even when my Latin teacher occasionally reprimanded me, "Böttger, why do Latin when you could lay paving stones for a living, always in the open air until you get old."

Now I experienced military drill I had never anticipated. We learned immediately to say a snappy " Jawohl!", "Achtung" and "zu Befehl", then we were chased around, ill-treated, ordered about, drilled and demoralized. We had to march for three hours wearing our gas masks constantly singing "It's so great to be a soldier. Annemarie" (*Es ist so schön, Soldat zu sein, Annemarie*), or were subjected to spiteful torment singly or in groups. During panzer training in the panzer hall one day, a recruit was told to put a magnetic lamp on the panzer. It fell off and he swore, "You clod!" The training corporal then ordered him to stand still, stroke the lamp and keep repeating, "I shall never call you a clod again."

An NCO had his quarters next to our squad room in the barracks. After he came off duty, if he wanted a beer or cigarettes from the canteen or his boots polished, or his jacket brushed and much else, then he would hammer the wall with his fist, and someone from the squad room had to knock on his door, reporting himself by name as a panzer soldier and await his task. Often there would be a disagreement between us squaddies as to who should go, maybe because the next man on our roster was not present, and then there would be a fierce discussion about who should substitute him always bearing in mind the cardinal rule "Never volunteer for anything". In the event of an undue delay in knocking at the NCO's door, the latter's sneering physiognomy would appear and demand, "Ach, I suppose nobody wants to do it?". Then he would begin to rant and rave, and we would be awarded a punishment such as: "Everybody out and line up with footstools held horizontally." A short while later we were on the floor, each holding a stool in stretched-out arms. Then he chased us through the barracks, ordering us from time to time, "Lay down!" or "Stand to attention!" As a closing flourish we had to crawl up the barrack stairs on our hands and knees holding the stool.

Another delightful reaction by this NCO, whose authority was based only on his collar lace, was a punishment known as "Sarassani" or "The Masked Ball." In this farce, the members of the squad room had to report first in fighting fatigues, then change quickly into grey uniform, then gym dress, then panzer uniform and finally walking-out uniform. This latter looked like a lion-tamer's get up with its colourful cuffs, braid and silver buttons, hence "Sarassani", from the circus of that name.

This inhuman tyranny naturally had nothing to do with military training or the realization of an ideology: it was much more the expression of an especially harsh and in many ways unworthy system of training soldiers. The Prussian military "virtues" such as precision, discipline and steadfastness were found here in unholy combination with Hitler's demand for the "best soldiers in the world". It was not difficult to imagine how the same bullying NCO, transplanted to the environment of a concentration camp, could very quickly turn executioner, intoxicated by the power he had inherited, the power of life and death.

Every squad-room inspection provoked anxiety and uncertainty. Everything which belonged to the barrack room, from the floor to tables and chairs, beds and lockers and the soldiers themselves would be inspected for cleanliness and good order. The beds would be checked not only to see that they had been "made", but that the blankets and pillows had been "boxed" exactly. We sprayed the chequered blanket covers with water to get them smooth and exact, but our bed-building frequently failed to please our platoon corporal or sergeant, or the *Spiess*, the company sergeant-major, the so-called "Mother of the Company". Then everything would fly – blankets, sheets and the straw from the mattresses.

Once on locker inspection I had to hold my shoes in my outstretched arms for a sergeant. He screamed, "You call them cleaned?" and immediately opened the window, throwing them to the courtyard three floors below. Another locker inspection I remember seeing was for ROB (Reserve Officer Applicant) soldiers, who had been selected for the officers' academy. They had to carry their heavy clothes lockers on their shoulders from the squad room down to the parade ground where they were be opened for inspection. By then the contents had naturally fallen into a confused tangle providing the corporal with many opportunities to demonstrate his power. In this way the young officer trainees, who in a short while would be giving their own orders to corporals, were "shown up". On leaving the squad room, the locker had to be locked. If it remained open, this created the disciplinary offence of "inducing theft by comrades".

For the first five months leave was granted only within a radius of fifty kilometres of the depot. At last the day came when I could apply for a leave pass, signed by the company commander, for a weekend in Freiburg. Once I got it, the evil corporal made me lie down on the earth with my rifle. Dust and dirt would always enter the barrel during this exercise, and checking the rifle for cleanliness afterwards he remarked, "There's a herd of elephants in the barrel". Therefore I had to clean the weapon, and time passed. The corporal was eventually satisfied with it and I sprinted to the station only to see the red rear lamps of the train disappearing into the distance. I cried with rage and frustration. A later request for leave was granted by the company commander, but bore corrections in red pencil. At school – as was then the custom – we had learned both the Old German and Latin scripts. I had developed a style in which I mixed them, and so though my application for leave was approved, the errors were highlighted in red. The purpose of the company commander was to show the *Abitur* student, the "nobody", that even after eight years of high school he was still unable to write German correctly.

Morning parade would often turn into a spiteful farce for the amusement of the *Spiess*. Should it be noticed that one's waist-belt or its buckle were not gleaming sufficiently, the collar of your tunic was not sitting quite right, or was not absolutely spotless, your hair was a shade too long or one was just an *Abiturient*, then there would follow the full package of punishments; lying down, knee bends, hopping like a hare or running around the barracks.

I remember especially a soldier, a small man in full marching order – rifle, backpack and steel helmet – who had to climb up a high box of sand placed outside the cellar windows as an air raid precaution. Once on top he had to stand to attention and shout, "I disgrace the German Wehrmacht", to which the cold-hearted *Spiess* would bellow "Louder!" This went on so long that the poor boy was almost hoarse repeating endlessly "I disgrace the German Wehrmacht". This small soldier on the sand box, terrified and near to tears, using the last of his energy to shout loud enough to please the *Spiess*, was a pitiful sight. This forced confession really was a disgrace to the German Wehrmacht.

I found punishments for bad shooting particularly unjust. Our company had done really poorly in panzer machine-gunnery. This was less the fault of the trainees than the task itself and the orders of the supervising corporal. An undulating concrete apron had a course marked out with flags. While driving a Panzer Mk I down the course, one had to fire twenty-five rounds at a target the full-size shape of a man. One's view of the outside world was obtained through a periscope. Now one can easily see that because the panzer rose and fell over the uneven concrete terrain, the barrel of the MG, a fixed installation in the turret, had a field of fire ranging between the concrete and the sky. I realized this when it was my turn to drive. I had long passed the first flag and now I was free to fire. Because I could not see the target I refrained from doing so. The corporal began shouting, "Will you bloody well fire!". I could still not see the target and thus held back. This was my first minor refusal to obey an order. Suddenly I saw the target perfectly positioned before the aiming spike of the periscope, depressed the foot-pedal and hit the target with every round of a 25-round burst. If I had obeyed "bloody well fire" and shot too soon, I would have discharged my rounds into the concrete or skywards just like the other recruits had done.

Because nearly all recruits had failed for the reason I have explained, we did not have to repeat the exercise but had punishment instead the following Sunday afternoon. This involved the 150 men of the recruit company assembling in a single file. The punishment began with the order "Quick march". Once the column was moving forward the platoon leaders would interject the order "Left about turn swivel march-march" or "Right about turn swivel march-march". Corresponding to the turn indicated, the soldier at the tail of the column had to do an about-turn on the spot. The next man up and the next right to the head of the line followed like the spokes of a wheel on an axis until all were walking or running backwards. Scarcely had the line reformed than came the next order "Twice left/right about turn march-march".

After four hours of this we were exhausted and in a great rage. The pithy words of our company commander, with which he had raised the spirits of his young recruits: "To be a recruit is the finest time of one's life" was very quickly seen as pure mockery.

On 30 March 1941 the recruits took their leave of the company commander with a big parade and much pomp. It was an occasion just like peacetime. Even in a garrison town like Böblingen, the war was still not being felt. After the strenuous training the little free time we had was spent writing letters and occasionally wandering the town on weekend leave. Mostly we went to cafés. Despite Hitler's wish that everybody should own a "people's radio", none of the recruits at Böblingen barracks had one. The highlight of our off-duty time was a visit to the cinema, at which the recruits would be enthusiastic at the UFA [State-owned film company] releases. Leaving the barracks the sentries would demand to see the soldier's paybook, a comb and a condom (particularly important because venereal disease was a punishable offence). Without these three items one could not pass the gate.

On 9 March 1941 we had leave to Stuttgart to see an international football match between Germany and Switzerland. It was especially enjoyable after weeks of barracks life to stroll past the well-cared-for shops on the König-Strasse. I recall particularly that apart from some good-looking girls almost every other pedestrian was an NCO or officer. This meant that one had to be eternally saluting every corporal, sergeant or officer whom one passed.

My time as a recruit was interrupted in the most pleasant way by the 5.Army Corps (Swabian Troops) ski championships held on the Feldberg in the Black Forest. One day the *Spiess* had asked if anybody could ski. My Freiburg friend from our RAD time stepped forward with me. Sent to the commanding officer's office we sensed at once the chance of a break from the harsh training and represented ourselves not only to be "experienced" Black Forest skiers, but also as members of a ski club of renown (Ski-Zunft Feldberg) and as such first-class cross-country men. In fact we had only ever taken part in training runs. Nevertheless we were sent to the championships and in the best March weather lodged for eight days at a Bärental pension at the foot of the Feldberg, did some skiing and basked frequently in the sun. Female friends visited us from Freiburg and in general a very good time was had by all. We took part in a kind of giant slalom. My starting number was 42 and I did not fall until very nearly at the finishing line. Only 72 of the 128 competitors completed the course. My friend also went down. Members of my unit also took part in the 4 x 5 km cross-country race.

During my recruit training I obtained the 10-tonne panzer driving permit. Instruction was given on a so-called LAS I or "farm tractor", these actually being cover-names from the time of the "black" Reichswehr, since it was actually a Panzer Mk I chassis. When recruit training finished at the end of March 1941, the majority of the men were posted to Pzr.Regts 7 or 8 in North Africa. I wrote to my mother about the successes of the German panzers in Africa and added my hope for a quick end to the war. We heard during training that Rommel would lead the Afrika Korps through Egypt to the Caucasus, and the German units fighting in the Balkans would come to meet him halfway. All Europe would then have been in the pincers of the German armies. One had only to look at the enormous distances on a map to doubt these predictions, however. Otherwise we never discussed the progress of the war. Now that I had the 10-tonne licence, in April 1941 I was posted to Putlos on the Baltic and after a four-week course obtained the driving permit – at just eighteen years of age – for tracked vehicles over 10 tonnes. This allowed me to drive a Panzer Mk III or IV.

On 1 June 1941 after six months' service in the Wehrmacht I was promoted to *Oberschütze* and wore a star on my left upper sleeve. The main boon of this was that curfew now ended for me at midnight instead of 2200 hrs. After another six months I became a *Gefreiter* (full private) and after two years six months an *Obergefreiter* (Senior private). This was not an NCO rank, but had the advantage that my pay went into a savings account in Swabia. Gross pay was 98 Reichsmarks per month (a soldier paid income tax and in winter a compulsory contribution to the *Winterhelfswerk* [Winter Relief charity]) so that after deductions an *Obergefreiter* was left with about 70 Reichsmarks as compared to an *Unteroffizier*, full corporal, the lowest NCO rank, who cleared 100 Reichsmarks.

Gefreiter and *Obergefreiter* were small steps up in the Wehrmacht hierarchy. They could give orders as squad-room leaders which had to be obeyed by *Schützen*, and could function as auxiliary instructors. (There was no equivalent rank of lance-corporal in the German Army, and although not an NCO, the *Obergefreiter* thus came nearest to it.). The standing of *Obergefreiter* before his superiors from corporal to field-marshal remained unchanged. With each higher rank in the Wehrmacht the power of command and the quality of the orders increased as did the number of subordinates. The highest rank still had the obligation both to give orders and to receive them. Only Hitler as supreme commander followed a different agenda. As dictator he had absolute power, but this was not God's gift from the bosom of the Church, for he saw himself called by Providence and given a mission.

At the front differences in rank were less important than fighting as a team under orders. On 22 June 1941 sitting near a radio I heard that German troops had marched into Russia. People still believed in a quick victory, although those who thought about it sensibly had their doubts, given the enormous size of the Soviet Union and *Abiturienten* remembered Napoleon's campaign in Russia from their history lessons: "With men and horse and wagons did God defeat him." That everything could get horribly worse nobody ever imagined.

Chapter 3

Transporter Missions

I was now a panzer driver and on 27 June 1941 was transferred to the OKH Panzer Reserve at Sagan in Silesia. This was a small garrison town on the Bober, a tributary of the Oder. Alongside exercises with the Mk III in the sandy pine forests around Sagan, the job of the panzer men there was to unload panzers arriving by train from the manufacturers and drive them to the barracks where to a certain extent they were held as "stock". When the need arose a certain number of panzers would be put aboard goods trains for fighting units in Russia, or to Italy for forwarding to North Africa.

Crews accompanying these machines were under the orders of OKH and after delivery had to return to Sagan. When I went once with a transport of that kind through Vyasma, about eighty kilometres short of Moscow, I experienced a Russian winter with temperatures of -40°C. Snow and ice on sections of the road were so hardened by the cold that on any incline the panzer tracks would fail to grip. Metal claws inserted in the tracks solved the problem. It was at Vyasma that I saw for the first time the bodies of Russian men and women lying frozen stiff at the sides of the road.

During the return journey to Sagan I had the doubtful pleasure of a delousing at Brest-Litovsk. In a special barracks hut all soldiers had to undress and hang their uniforms and underclothing on a frame. The clothing was then deloused in a gas chamber while the soldiers had to shower scrupulously with soap and hot water. This had to be repeated, and we begged a cooking pot full of hot water from a locomotive driver. After that we sat in a waiting room until we received back our deloused clothing.

On another transport mission I went with a Sagan squad to Brindisi in southern Italy. This extremely interesting trip lasted four days. When the train stopped at Plauen in the Vogtland one of the Red Cross nurses on duty on the station gave me a gramophone and fifty records donated by the local population. I did not like any of the records except one by a French singer: "*J'attendrai, le jour et la nuit j'attendrai toujours...*" I played this record without a break until we got to Brindisi, where we drove the panzers off the train into an orchard with fig trees.

The next day it snowed, then the Italians went on strike – our allies in the midst of a war – and they refused to load our panzers aboard ship. This forced us to reload them on the train and travel down to Naples. We did not mind this for it gave us the chance to "see Naples and die" (but only when we were old). In Naples we stayed in an hotel near the train station. At last we had a proper bed again, and in no time at all we felt that the war could never be better than this for us. Since there was nothing to do in the next few days we went to Vesuvius and also Pompeii where I saw in the original a Janus head which I already knew from my Latin book *Ludus Latinus*.

We were especially impressed by a wall painting where a man had painted his sexual member in the form of a large fish on a balance, weighing it against gold. Our curiosity led us to hire an official guide who promised more erotic scenes, and so we got to see the nooks "where the woman snuffs out the candle". Women and eroticism were the predominant scene. Thus in Naples we went to a soldiers' brothel such as Wehrmacht High Command had set up everywhere in rear areas. At first we thought it was a café but soon noticed the difference. Our corporal promised us a special show with a prostitute. A young soldier was picked and we were supposed to watch but since he could not do it with an audience the corporal chased us all out of the room and did it himself. We liked seeing the foreplay but not the completion.

Most soldiers of my age were much too young anyway for such "café visits". A sort of hierarchy not based on military rank reigned there. As a rule young recruits and soldiers lacked sexual experience. Those who did not were listened to with respect when they described their relationships with women, sexual experiences and practices. We had left school and our parental home unenlightened. Now we wanted our share of it and to hear more about "Subject No.1" every day and gain experience, not only by talking about it but finally making up for what we had missed, and we were aching to start. On the other hand, however, we were mortally afraid of infection and the disgrace of at least 21 days imprisonment for contracting gonorrhoea, and this cooled our passions.

The Sagan squad loafed around Naples for more or less ten days. We liked the city very much and took many photos, even some of the port installations despite the ban on doing so. When the happy time came to an end we were given Afrika Korps uniforms to transport the panzers there and – as was originally intended – to join Rommel. Unusually we were offered the choice of going to North Africa or returning to Sagan. The officer was probably ordered! One man decided for Africa, the rest of us preferred Sagan. Later I met this would-be Afrika Korps panzer man. He related that his ship, loaded with our panzers, was torpedoed and sunk in the Gulf of Naples. He swam away from the vessel but had serious facial burns.

Each of us brought back to Sagan a large, cumbersome wooden box with our purchases. Mine contained two silk shirts which I purchased at a gentleman's outfitter. Despite the war his stock was little different from what he sold in peacetime. We took the express train for soldiers on leave from the front (SF 568) which left Naples daily at 0754 hrs and arrived at 1658 hrs the next day at Berlin-Anhalter. The route passed through Rome where it was forbidden to alight – the city was barred to German soldiers in transit – to Munich, and after several changes of train with our boxes we arrived at Sagan and had the usual 45-minute march from the station to the Dachsberg barracks. We put the boxes on a van.

On a short driving course at Wünsdorf I trained with a group of drivers over very hilly terrain. With the control stick one could operate the left and right tracks individually or together, declutch, disconnect or apply the brakes. Thus the control stick could be used to steer the panzer in various directions. To avoid zigzagging, the driver had to develop a fine touch. It gave me great pleasure to drive a Mk IV from the training depot at Neuhammer down an inclined section of the autobahn at 82 kms/hr. This enormous speed with rattling caterpillar tracks was intoxicating.

Off duty I used to play tennis at the Sagan club not only with other soldiers and officers but mainly with club members. I made the acquaintance of several very respected inhabitants of the town and received a number of invitations as though it were peacetime. On 12/13 September 1942 a competition was held between the Sagan club (Saganer SV) and TV 1861 Cottbus. A mixed team made the trip to Cottbus. By "mixed" I mean not only the mixed doubles (ladies and gentlemen) but primarily the men's team which consisted of officers, NCOs, panzer men and civilians. I had fallen in love with my tennis partner Karin, but had to recognize however that the "little private" did not quite measure up, and I never saw her again after a short stay at Sagan in 1944.

Pretty Anita who worked in a photo shop supplied me with monochrome and colour film (2 RM and 3.50 RM respectively). A member had a very large collection of records, and so I got used to listening to music. People said after the war that many musicians and conductors such as B. W. Furtwängler put themselves in the service of the Nazis and were therefore responsible to some extent for encouraging enthusiasm for the war in many Germans. In those days a concert could not reach a great majority of the people, there was no television, not many had a radio, gramophones and records were a rarity. For someone fighting at the front it was just not possible to have Furtwängler's Beethhoven or a monumental rendering by Breker (*Die Kameraden* or *Die Vergeltung*) to whip up one's heroism or take music or art for its own sake into battle. During the fighting all that mattered was survival. The soldiers I knew were rarely interested in classical music.

Certainly Prussian military marches had the suggested effect: there was something soldierly and snappy with the hurly-burly of victory about them, and for the average German a reminder of the Kaiser's epoch, an era of splendour. As a soldier I loved to follow a behind a military band playing a march through a small village, but it ended there.

What really interested a soldier was food – he had a permanent ravenous hunger – and insofar as they were available, women. He liked to have his rest and plenty of leave. Basically what kept him going was food, drink and women. Education in the Wehrmacht was a non-starter. One could buy books which would be useful in this respect but they were rarely read. Quite different motives played a major role in maintaining morale during the fighting: activities with the single objective of winning a decoration. A medal on the jacket pocket was the visible proof to all and sundry that here was a man who had fought bravely. I knew commanders who could not rest until they had destroyed a certain number of enemy tanks, which would earn them the Iron Cross, and then they would aim for the Knight's Cross.

Back to the main interest of all soldiers, food. In a letter to my mother dated 1 October 1941 from Sagan I wrote: "In the mornings I eat only two slices of bread because that is all there is. The daily ration is 500 grams of bread. At midday I stuff myself until I can take no more, i.e. ten to fifteen potatoes. Nevertheless I am always ravenous, and ten minutes later I could eat a loaf of bread. But in a large garrison town like Sagan one cannot find a meal off ration. On Sundays the menu appears with two or three dishes struck out, and if you want something in particular you have to be in the shop queue by 10.15." This anxiety about food was the main theme of the letters to my mother. Often I begged her to send me money to buy something edible in the local shops. There was no shortage of cigarettes, especially the brands NIL and JUNO, nor of toilet articles such eau-de-cologne or toothpaste.

During this time at Sagan the soldiers' bread ration was reduced further. To prevent my being plagued by hunger, now and again my mother sent me some coupons from her ration book. On the way to the tennis courts, the road passed a baker's shop. I had flirted wildly with the assistant and looked deeply into her eyes. This paid off because she gave me bread without coupons. Unfortunately a few weeks later she just happened to be looking out of a window at the rear of the shop and saw me kissing another girl in front of the tennis courts. The next time I came in she hardly acknowledged me and my coupon-free era of bread and cakes was over.

In the mornings, occasionally I went for a training hour on the officers' tennis courts at the barracks. The company commander took me in his Cabriolet from there to the Sagan tennis club where we played as a doubles pair. I was a very good doubles player and we won regularly, much to the joy of the *Oberstleutnant*. These special privileges did not escape the beady eyes of my immediate superiors from squad-room corporal up to the *Spiess*, and when one of my tennis-playing officers obtained a special leave for me, the *Spiess* warned: "You think you're getting an extra sausage. But you will hardly reach home and your arse won't have warmed before you get the order to return to your unit." He did what he could to make that come true, his idea being to transfer me out at once to the front. It just so happened, however, that a medical officer diagnosed a stomach ulcer from which I had been suffering for some time. I was reclassified as *garnisonsverwendungsfähig* (fit for garrison duty only), and the *Spiess* was foiled. He "boiled over"!

In October 1942 a section of my company was sent to Rothenburg in Silesia for the potato harvest. A Lanz-Bulldog tractor did the rounds of a large field towing a potato-unearthing machine. It passed us every ten minutes and we had to gather up the potatoes it tossed out. To an extent we were forced labourers, and worked together with Italian male and female farmhands and also French PoWs. Alongside our group of soldiers and working with us were thirty Jews identified by a yellow star on the left breast. Most of them were women, and one could see that in the past they had known better times, for the majority wore fine ski-suits. The work was hard, not least because of the occasional inclement weather. In snow showers, rain and frost the fingers suffered the worst. We had to dig potatoes from 0700 to 1830 hrs, with one hour off for lunch at midday.

As compensation for this grind we were very well fed. Once we even got roast venison with cabbage and gravy and, of course, potatoes. Now and again we stole apples and soon had enough to send a parcel of them home. In November that same year we harvested beet. Here again we were unused to this unpleasant work, especially since November was so cold. On the other hand it was preferable to harvest beet than fight on the Russian Front. Near the front line after an exhausting advance there was that extreme cold which I had experienced on the Vyasma rail transport and which a sergeant returning from there described to us.

In January 1943 ski training was introduced at Panzerersatzabteilung (Panzer Reserve Battalion) 15 at Sagan. OKH was not certain that there would be enough panzers available, therefore panzer men had to learn how to fight as infantry in snow. We exercised with skiers, running, attacking and shooting. On a weekend leave pass I went to the Riesengebirge in Silesia via Krummhübel twice for alpine skiing. It was a difficult journey; from Sagan we had to change four times at Soran, Kohlfurt, Lauban and Hirschberg before we even got to Krummhübel.

I befriended a sergeant and we lodged at the Bergheil pension, where the food was coupon-free. We went up to a small pond above the

Hampelbaude and joyfully did some real skiing. A short time later the sergeant was transferred to officers' training where he shot himself in the hand during weapons cleaning but still emerged from the Academy as a lieutenant.

At the beginning of February 1943 I had to report to the company commander supposedly because I was to be transferred. In fact it was for a skiing course (10 February 1943) at Kronstadt via Habelschwerdt in the Silesian Glatzer-Bergland. They were trying out the Army flat-country binding there which corresponded to the modern long-distance binding in its principle of movement. The normal shoe fitted inside a leather over-shoe fastened through two eyelets to the ski toe-piece. This binding, which was suitable for all skis, provided an outstanding cross-country performance. It was naturally unsuitable for downhill work.

On 18 February 1943 in a major propaganda event at the Berlin Sportpalast, Goebbels made his famous speech about the ten so-called "Questions concerning the destiny of the German Volk". Present were wounded men from the Eastern Front, Knight's Cross holders, Oak Leaves holders, armaments workers, soldiers, surgeons, scientists, artists, engineers, architects, teachers, Party functionaries, officials, employees and thousands of German women.

Goebbels began by saying: "Therefore I can justly claim that what I see seated before me is a cross-section of the entire German people from the front and Homeland. Is that right?" At the moment the question was put, the Sportpalast experienced a demonstration of fanatical support which this old stadium of the National Socialist struggle can only have known at especial highpoints of its story. The mass sprang up out of their seats as though electrified. Like a hurricane, "Ja!" roared out from the many thousands of voices. This response was meant to mimic a referendum and the expression of the People's free will, and could not have been conjured up in a more spontaneous manner.

Another quote from this speech was: "Therefore you, my listeners, represent the nation at this moment in time, and I would like to address ten questions to you, to which you should give me the answers on behalf of the German people before the whole world, but especially before our enemies, who are also listening at their radios." The he asked the ten questions, following each of which, each time, the audience jumped up and gave their approval as if in a single voice. The most portentous of these questions was: "Do you want total war?" This question, too, was acclaimed with tumultuous jubilation.

It was about this time that ever more soldiers, including those from my own circle of acquaintances, began to die. The war had begun to come threateningly closer. One of the first to fall was the well-known Freiburg skier Richard Cranz, followed by many of my colleagues from school and the Hitler Youth.

I was granted home leave from Panzerersatzabteilung 15 at Sagan. The railway journey to Freiburg was tiring and involved many changes but – with my home leave pass in my pocket – was the fulfillment of happiness for the soldier. Cottbus, Frankfurt an der Oder, Halle, Dresden was the route the train followed. Generally one would be directed to take the SF (fast train for leave-takers from the front) or DmW, EmW or PmW (public trains with Wehrmacht coaches attached), but if one was lucky a railway officer might approve travel by normal express.

During these journeys and at the stations, Feldgendarmes [military police] constantly monitored the leave-takers. We soldiers called them "chained dogs" from the inverted half-moon metal plaque with engraved eagle resting on the chest and attached to chains around their neck. They checked travel warrants and tickets and would occasionally open one's gasmask canister to make sure it contained the gas mask and not sandwiches. During such a leave journey, I visited my uncle Albert Böttger at Leipzig. On 14 February 1924 he had founded a home there where socially disadvantaged young persons or those with learning disabilities could be trained in horticulture, woodwork, metalwork, domestic and building economy and generally receive trade training. Despite his great success, my uncle was removed by the Nazis, and the standard of living of the mentally deficient fell to primitive levels. After the capitulation my uncle was reinstated by the DDR as the head of the school at Leipzig which now bears his name.

Chapter 4

The Death Sentence

There was a panzer man at the Dachsberg Barracks at Sagan who came from my neighbourhood in Freiburg. Well-appointed by Nature, tall and well developed with wonderful blond hair, he was well known to the boys and above all the girls at home. I saw him occasionally with his brother when we were both serving with the same *Jungvolk* unit.

An Order of the Day described how he had planned to survive the war by improper means. His story came in three acts. In the first act he was serving a short sentence in the barracks cells. One night he escaped, broke into the company office and a sergeant's room, where he stole a pistol, Wehrmacht documents and a rubber stamp used for official purposes. Then he made off and disappeared from sight.

The second act was played out in the centre of Leipzig. A good-looking Luftwaffe officer, decorated and with a bandaged head, came walking down the street. "A heroic aviator" many must have thought immediately at the sight of him. A sergeant, also from Freiburg and the same neighbourhood, addressed the aviator: "Hallo, D--, what are you doing here?" The Luftwaffe man then made the biggest mistake of his life by reprimanding the sergeant. "Who are you to speak to me with familiarity? I don't know you, clear off!" The sergeant obeyed but realized that something was amiss, for he definitely recognized the young man and felt sure that the other knew him. He could have let the matter slip, but notified the Feldgendarmerie instead. The Luftwaffe man's papers were checked and identified as forgeries. The head bandage was a mock-up. The deserter panzer man was unmasked. That night he dug a hole in his cell wall but not deep enough to escape.

The third act played out at Sagan. At morning parade the *Spiess* read out an Order of the Day: Panzer soldier D-- had been reduced to the ranks and sentenced to die by firing squad. The execution was scheduled for that same afternoon in a pine forest on the outskirts of Sagan. Then the *Spiess* read out the names of the firing party. I could have attended the execution as a witness. The *Spiess* allowed any soldier who wished to attend to travel by official lorry to the place of execution, but I had not desire to see the spectacle.

Upon their return the witnesses reported that D-- had shown no fear. It was a strange situation. He who had wanted to escape a soldiers' death in action by deserting now stared death in the face. His hands bound to a stake, with an elegant toss of his head he shook off his forage cap from his blond head as the firing party took aim. Then came the order to fire and he was hit. One might almost say he died like a hero. And because he told the firing squad "Don't shoot me in the face," one might also say that he died a beautiful hero.

Thus this young soldier, who had hoped to survive the war away from the front, finished up by achieving exactly what he most wanted to avoid: to die like a hero. For the witnesses this hour of execution was one of those demonstrations of the power of the Hitler-State which insisted ruthlessly on discipline and obedience and had a deserter shot without mercy even in May 1945 when the war was obviously lost. We young soldiers had now been shown where disobedience to orders and deserting the colours led.

Nowadays we armchair critics would condemn the death penalty in cases such as those of D-- as brutal and unjust, but in the era of the Wehrmacht another outlook and feelings prevailed which do not bear comparison with those of today. We soldiers sitting in our squad-room were appalled to hear what one of the witnesses related; not only the death of one of our own, but of his execution nearby. Though horrified we made no criticism of the sentence, however. Inwardly we accepted what had been hammered into us in training: "This is what happens to a deserter." Thus we directed our criticism at the brashness and stupidity of D--. With all the permanent Wehrmacht controls, not to mention watchful district superintendents and Gestapo agents in housing blocks in the home province, escape and disguise as a "Luftwaffe officer" was a poor idea.

Chapter 5

I Join 24.Panzer Division in France

My stay with transport unit Panzerersatzabteilung 15 lasted two years because of a string of illnesses from which I suffered including jaundice, stomach disorders and a carbuncle. These required visits to the field hospital where the medical officer wrote me down "GvH" (*garnisonsverwendungsfähig Heimat* – fit only for garrison duty, Homeland.) When one recalls that meanwhile the war was going full out and Hitler had ordered that every soldier should be at the front fighting, then my hour of posting to a fighting unit came relatively late in my career as a soldier.

After my departure from Sagan, a Staff NCO wrote to my mother: "Arnim has now left, and I went with him to the station. I would happily have gone the whole way, but I received my own orders to joing SA-Standarte *Feldherrnhalle.*" This letter shows that a soldier seldom had influence in determining to which unit he should be sent, and he could be transferred out of a Wehrmacht unit into the SS or SA. In the last days of the war I also landed up with this former SA outfit, now called Panzerkorps *Feldherrnhalle.* All the same, possibilities did become available even in wartime to make daily life more bearable under the prevailing circumstances, and influence one's path as a soldier, albeit within very narrow limits. One needed the will and courage to go for it, and be ready to assume certain risks in order to take one's fate back into one's own hands. I shall describe this later.

On 5 April 1943 I arrived in France where a new unit was being formed. My leave-taking was a tearful affair, the last act being a march from the barracks to Sagan railway station preceded by a military band playing "The Hour of Departure" and the Faust waltz by Berlioz, this latter rendered in a very racy manner. On the station platform my friend *Unteroffizier* Graf Posadowsky-Wehner[1] invited me into the compartment he was occupying. There was a sign on the sliding door: "Reserved for *Wachtmeister*". I said at once, "Man, Heynco, I am a private soldier, I can't sit in a compartment

---

1. His uncle was a Secretary of State and from 1897 to 1907 Deputy Reich Chancellor. As a German Nationalist he opposed Friedrich Ebert in the election for Reich President at the National Assembly in Weimar.

Tanks in both World Wars: German soldiers pose before a British Mark IV, late First World War.

Panzer Mk IV of the Wehrmacht, the most numerous German panzer type, mid-Second World War.

By car (Bergman) to the frontline (1916). My father is in the back seat.

A visit to an army headquarters by my father during the First World War.

From high school desk to the RAD: no more Latin, the important thing now is felling trees on the estates of the Prince of Thurn und Taxis.

Inspection of boots and uniform by a beady-eyed RAD officer, checking here to ensure all hob-nails are present and correct on the sole. The haversack contains all the worldly possessions of these workers with spades.

Curiosity and admiration. Townspeople of Freiburg/Breisgau look over two 15-cm self-propelled assault guns in the Tal-Strasse in 1940 after the French campaign.

Panzer training: a training NCO aboard a Panzer I on the training ground at Böblingen.

Car wash duty on an Opel Olympia. The rectangular insignia on the left mudguard indicates a panzer regiment. In the background are the panzer barracks at Böblingen.

5.Army Corps ski championships, on the Feldberg (Black Forest). The Böblingen panzer ski team at the start of the 4 x 5km cross-country race, the "Feldberger Hof" hotel in the background.

Gunnery training on a Mk I over an undulating concrete surface.

Training school for the 10 tonnes + panzer driving permit: the author changed to this larger tank, Mk IV (model A) with short-barrelled gun, for training at Putlos.

Walking-out dress, Prussian style: the unpopular and uncomfortable "Sarassani", so-called after the circus of the same name.

Partial view of the Dachsberg barracks at Sagan, Silesia, occupied today by the Polish Army. Little has changed except for a T-34 on the roundabout as a memorial: the eagle and swastika over the entrance have naturally been removed.

The Bober bridge at Sagan, destroyed in 1945.

reserved for sergeants upwards." He replied with a superior air, "I already have my own seat here, and if any of them protest about you being here I shall give them a few eggs.," He had an estate in Silesia and food aplenty. The sergeants accepted the eggs and no protests arose. Graf Posadowsky, an urbane figure in all circumstances, knew how to bring people under his spell. As the train headed for France, several WOIIs, a corporal and a private all played Skat harmoniously.

The soldiers transferred with me filled two trainloads. We went via Dresden to the Rhine at Worms, then crossed the border. Finally we reached our destination at Brionne in Normandy and drew private billets. No panzers were there and we had to make do with two captured French tanks for training purposes.

I practised my schoolboy French with a salesgirl in a small shop. She was very pretty and the French chatter did at least result in my being able to buy a good quantity of herbs and spices, which I sent home at once. A few souvenir photos of this time remain. In general French women avoided being seen with German soldiers in public. After a few days the unit moved on to Epaignes, population 800, eleven kilometres from Port Audemer and twenty-five from Lisieux. There the panzers arrived. These turned out to be self-propelled assault guns (SP-guns).

The new 24.Pzr.Div. was to be formed and trained at Epaignes. It was made up of the East Prussian 1.Kavallerie-Div., which had fought in Poland, France and Russia, while 24.Pzr.Regt was composed of Reiter (Cavalry) Regt.2 and 26. In recognition of the glorious history of the German cavalry, on 25 October 1941 the then Commander-in-Chief of the Army, *Feldmarschall* von Brauchitsch, had authorized that the reformed 24.Pzr.Div. could continue to wear the gold piping on cap, collar and shoulder straps. All other German panzer men had pink piping (communications troops wore bright yellow).

Corresponding to the terminology used in mounted regiments, "*Rittmeister*" replaced the rank *Hauptmann* (captain), "*Wachtmeister*" replaced *Feldwebel* (sergeant), and the Company was known as a "*Schwadron*" (squadron). The divisional sign displayed on every vehicle was also in the cavalry tradition: rider and mount clearing a hurdle. This special regulation documented the fact that the newly formed division was a traditional unit of the Army. In a leaflet dropped by Soviet aircraft, 24.Pzr.Div. was called "the bloodhounds of Voronezh". This did not refer to any atrocity perpetrated by the division but to its rapid advance into the city after crossing the Don in July 1942.

Von Senger und Etterlin wrote in his book on 24.Pzr.Div. that the division had played a special role in the pursuit of the Soviet troops. On 17 or 18 June 1942 it had crossed the great bend in the Don with the intention of appearing in the Caucasus as a strong panzer spearhead. This failed because of a shortage of fuel. The war history has not clearly apportioned blame for the failure, but according to H. G. Dahms, Hitler identified *Feldmarschall* von Bock as the culprit and relieved him of command. Subsequently 24.Pzr.Div. bled to death at Stalingrad. Those parts of the division outside the encirclement, and those men wounded or for other reasons stationed in Germany, now formed the core of the reconstituted division.

My squadron commander, *Oberleutnant* Hupe, had the job of getting us accustomed to the SP-gun which he succeeded in doing with Prussian determination and discipline. Now at last it no longer came as a hard and senseless drill as I experienced while a recruit at Böblingen, but as the correct and necessary training.

The Sturmgeschütz III (variant G) had a crew of four, contrary to the Panzer Mk III or IV with which I had been familiar at Sagan. The turret had little rotational movement so that the SP-gun had to face the target frontally to fire with the cannon or MG. (The chassis was the same as the Panzer Mk III with six wheels; the gun was a 7.5-cm/L48 long barrelled weapon.)

For encouragement a Wehrmacht entertainment troupe visited us. An orchestra accompanied a colourful programme including female dancers. One of them sang, "Michael, am I not the girl for you?". Definitely, thought the majority of the audience, even if not one of us was called Michael.

On another occasion while walking off-duty I tried out my schoolboy French on a young French woman. What I knew was sufficient, and it was one of those rare moments in a soldier's life when something he was taught at school turned out to have some use. We discussed only everyday things but I had the impression that to her I was more than just a pleasant passing acquaintance. She ran a small souvenir shop in Lisieux and although it was forbidden I cycled via Cormeilles, where a neighbouring squadron was stationed, to Lisieux. Following my promotion to *Obergefreiter* I considered myself a long-serving soldier who in having to choose between the yearning for a new love and orders not to absent myself from Epaignes could decide for myself in favour of the former.

Quickly I found the gift shop close to the church at Lisieux. I propped my bicycle against the house wall and entered (21 May 1943). After my initial *Bonjour madame* we looked each other in the eyes in the shadows. She was dreadfully nervous, gave me the present of a talisman, and then I remounted my bicycle in the hope of returning to Epaignes unseen. We had agreed to correspond and so I gave her my address, telling her she should send a letter to me at Epaignes with the everyday French post endorsed "To be called for". She could also give her letter to a German

soldier but in that case she must only use my field-post number 46780E –
and nothing else – as the address.

Either she did not understand these two ways of addressing the letter
or desired it to arrive in my hands faster and more surely by having the
fullest address possible. A few days later the *Spiess* ordered me at morning
parade: "*Obergefreiter* Böttger, 1200 hours, commander, steel helmet!" A
summons phrased in this way boded ill. Anybody could see from it that
something serious had occurred, something which was likely to result in
my being thrown into a cell somewhere.

My friend Graf Posadowsky spoke perfect French. Before I reported,
the squadron commander gave him a letter addressed to me. On the
envelope was an address in which "Epaignes" and the field-post number
appeared together. From my "either – or" the French girl had gone instead
for "this as well as that". Posadowsky translated the letter. It began with
"My dearest Armin" and related the passion of young love. Posadowsky
was able to give me a brief indication and so I knew what the problem
was when I entered the commander's office at midday wearing my steel
helmet, clicked my heels and reported myself present.

I was accused of a breach of security. The location of a field-post number
had to be kept strictly secret. A dour interrogation followed. After hearing
Posadowsky's translation, the squadron commander recognized that this
was a harmless love-letter and in principle no military secret had been
compromised. Thus I came away with a reprimand. In future letters my
French girlfriend told me that she was going to take a German conversation
course, and finally she visited me at Epaignes after writing: "Another three
days separate us, one from the other, how long that is!"

At Epaignes RAF fighters often flew over dropping leaflets. Later they
machine-gunned the village. Then came air raids by RAF and USAF
bombers. The flak got one. Three men baled out and on bicycles we had to
search for them. We found one. He had a broken leg. His parachute was
of the finest silk which impressed me enormously. I also liked his flying
suit. He had chocolate and amphetamines on his person. A few days later
150 four-engined bombers passed overhead at low level but failed to see
us. That night an RAF fighter spotted a light and opened fire with his 2-cm
cannons. A sleeping corporal was hit in the leg.

For gunnery training we drove our SP-guns to a military depot near
Falaise where we spent the night in tents. The exercise with the cannons
was held in a potato field. Afterwards we had to collect up the potatoes
which had been unearthed during the shelling. In the evening our gun
crew went out hoarding.

Once we visited the well-known sea resorts of Trouville and Deauville.
We went by lorry to a small stretch of beach open to bathers. The big

promenade hotels in Deauville were deserted and partially camouflaged. Grass and weeds a metre high grew on the many tennis courts. The Trouville casino was closed, of course, but the restaurants were open, and served lobster, oyster, sole and roast beef without any restrictions. For a soldier at war a glorious but very rare excursion! On to Rouen, where many cafés were intact and ice cream, strawberries, peaches and cherries could be had – I went there to be measured for new spectacles by a Wehrmacht optician.

Occasionally the squadron would have a get-together at which the alcohol would flow. Festivities were embellished by a corporal who played the accordion for our entertainment, one of his favourites being the British wartime hit, "We're going to hang out our washing on the Siegfried Line". He was a great character. It was said he had a Jewish grandfather, but this was not of any interest to us.

In the endless days exercising with the SP-gun I had noticed that the "poor bastard" in the crew was the driver. He was always in action, especially when driving, while the rest of those aboard, apart from the commander, were more or less only along for the ride.

Quite to my surprise, on 8 June 1943 I was sent from France with a few others for a course at Neisse in Silesia (3 K-Bat. Sturmgeschützersatzabteilung 300 [3K Battery Assault Gun Battalion 300]). It was for special training in something or other but when we got to Neisse the place was in chaos and nobody knew what to do with us. The opportunity cropped up unexpectedly for me to do a radio operator's course. I volunteered at once for I liked the idea of exchanging the driving seat for the radioman's seat as soon as possible.

To start off one had to learn Morse code. I knew this already from my training with the *Jungvolk*. The principal aim of instruction was the new method of spoken communication between individual panzers and panzer crews. It required no special skill. On the journey to Neisse my comrades and I took advantage of a half day in Paris to see the sights. From the Arc de Triomphe with its eternal flame on the memorial to the Unknown Soldier, and its famous inscription *Ici répose un soldat francais mort por la patrie,* we walked the Champs Élysées, past the Grand Palais and over the Seine bridge to the Invalides cathedral. I liked Paris very much and took photos of the streets and buildings from one end of the walk to the other. Below the memorial to Napoleon three panzer men posed for a group photo. They were still dreaming of panzer victories then, and little did they know that their own Waterloo lay before them.

Back at Epaignes I no longer drove the SP-gun and was reassigned as a radio operator. The longer we remained in France the more the rumours abounded that we would soon be at the front. Obviously we knew that a strong operational panzer regiment would not sit out the war in France.

Talk of an imminent move to Italy grew after we were allowed a short home leave. I went to Freiburg via Strasbourg.

W. Warlimont (see *Bibliography*) reported from FHQ (Führer HQ – Hitler's field headquarters) on the reasons for the transfer to Italy. According to the official record of a situation conference on 25 July 1943, Hitler said: "Therefore in principle one panzer division, that is the 24th, is ready. The most important thing is that 24.Pzr.Div. is moved at once to south of the Brenner, so that 24.Pzr.Div. passes through there immediately on any of the railway lines and is concentrated there immediately allowing Grenadier-Div. *Feldherrnhalle* to at least control the crossings." Later there was this exchange:

Hitler: "The first five divisions are therefore there, is 24.Pzr.Div. there yet?"

Jodl: "24.Pzr.Div. is also there."

Hitler: "It must go in there, that is quite certain."

At the situation conference of 27/28 December 1943 Hitler asked, "What is the state of 24 Pzr.Div.?"

Zeitzler: "Threre is no full assessment, but it is strong. Fighting value 1."

At the beginning of August 1943 we learned officially of our transfer to Italy and a couple of days later we boarded the train for the Army Equipment Office at Magdeburg, the centre responsible for the supply of weapons, vehicles, equipment and new formations. We left the SP-guns in France and at Magdeburg took possession of our new Panzer Mk IV variant F, 25 tonnes heavy with additional armour on the so-called "front skirt". We were left bemused at the thinking behind our training to date, for the Panzer Mk IV was of quite different construction to the SP-gun with which we had worked up. Beside the turret, which could be turned by handwheel or by a 600 cc. two-stroke motor, the crew consisted of five men (commander, driver, gunner, loader and radio operator). The panzer itself was seven metres long overall and 3.33 metres wide and in contrast to the Mk III had eight wheels per side. It was powered by a 320-hp Maybach petrol motor which gave a range of 130 to 150 kilometres cross-country on a full tank of 470 litres. The main armament was a 7.5-cm long barrelled gun and an MG in the turret, a second ball-mounted MG with an armoured shield was operated by the radio operator.

Chapter 6

Second Class Soldiers?

T he central pillar of Adolf Hitler's policy was the persecution of the Jews. The NSDAP programme stipulated that a Jew could not be a German citizen. The Nuremberg racial laws prescribed that a full Jew was a person with at least three Jewish grandparents. A person of mixed blood of the second degree had one or two full blood Jewish grandparents. In rare cases, a person of the second degree could wear the Wehrmacht uniform. The former Federal Chancellor Helmut Schmidt spoke in a television programme in March 1995 of his Jewish grandfather. He had only been told about him by his parents after he declared his intention to join the Hitler Jugend. "We used falsified documents to survive throughout the Third Reich," Schmidt explained. He became an officer in the flak, and so important was his position in Germany's air defence system that he even managed to dodge proceedings against himself "because of my big mouth". Two Luftwaffe generals helped him in this. There were two panzer men with a similar anamnesis in 12.Sq/24.Pzr.Regt, and I shall now describe how they handled the problem.

During my service with Panzerersatzabteilung 15 at Sagan, I got to know Unteroffizier Heynco Graf Posadowsky-Wehner. We were immediately on the same wavelength and a very close friendship developed. He was a well-educated man with an estate in Silesia and spoke the foreign languages English, French, Italian and Polish. Accordingly, he assumed for himself a leading role in the unit. Other soldiers who met him, from the squadron commander to the knotty-hearted *Spiess* to the lowest loader, were fascinated by his personality. We stuck together on and off duty. We took countless walks from the barracks across the Bober bridge at Sagan. For Party members the important thing about my friend Heynco was that he had a Jewish grandmother and was therefore of "impure race". So far as 12.Squadron was concerned this was irrelevant. Never once did I hear any man in the squadron mention it, nor did Heynco ever experience any difficulties at Sagan because of it. Our common path ran from Panzerersatzabteilung 15 as far as the first action with 24.Pzr.Div. in Russia, where we seaparated. He went to the War Academy and obtained his commission.

If one recalls that at the end of 1916 during the First World War the recriminations against Jews increased, and as a result in the Prussian Army no more Jews were promoted to officer, then Posadowsky's achievement in a monstrous State such as the Third Reich was must point to something extraordinary. One must suppose that in his case special considerations came into play to smooth the way to officer. As Leutnant Posadowsky I met him once briefly at Sagan in September 1944. After the war I received from his son, who had been too young to know his father, two letters from his comrades who shared the last hours of Posadowsky's life. One letter stated that on 15 August 1945 the count died in a train at Kohlfurt (Silesia) while on the way to a discharge station at Görlitz in East Prussia. As the result of general physical debility, when so close to his dream of reunion with his beloved wife and two children, of whom he spoke so often, he was denied it. He was buried by his comrades not far from the goods yard at Kohlfurt (branch line near Görlitz). The writer of the letter went on to say that Posadowsky had been captured by the Soviets at Halbe on 28 or 29 April 1945. Wounded in the knee, he was taken by train from Tschenstochau to a military hospital where he suffered an amputation at the thigh. The wound did not heal well; although otherwise in good health his strength slowly ebbed, accelerated by pneumonia. His belongings, a silver cigarette case and gold engagement ring with a diamond, were stolen by a Russian female officer at the hospital. In the colour photo in this book, this engagement ring can be clearly seen on the ring finger of the right hand next to the wedding ring. The second letter said much the same except for the allegation that Posadowsky had always had difficulties in the Third Reich on account of his Jewish grandmother.

In France, Heynco and I had been joined in friendship by *Unteroffizier* Achim Dohany, who had obtained his *Abitur* and was already six years a soldier on the defensive – he had a Jewish grandfather.

During peacetime Dohany joined Reiter-Regt 2 as a conscript. When his time was up after two years the war arrived and so he had to stay in. He was an excellent comrade and on the basis of many interests in common there arose at Epaignes a triple friendship. His mother lived at Buchheim near Freiburg, and, advised of this in our field letters home, his mother and mine telephoned and met regularly to chat about their sons and keep up with the news. Achim used to carry an accordion in his pack and would play for our entertainment and relaxation at squadron get-togethers. He had a peculiar repertoire which included snappy-style German marches and then English hit melodies. He wrote a memoir describing his career in the military entitled "Second Class Soldier":

In 1935 my father placed a bottle of cognac within his reach and suggested I should attend to the potatoes. When I returned some time later the bottle was empty and my father was very merry. In my absence he had rung all the cavalry regiments and discovered that his own regimental comrade Göschen was commanding Reiter-Regt 2 in East Prussia. He told me he had applied on my behalf. When I entered it in 1937 as a 20-year-old, Göschen had been replaced by von Saucken, later a general and holder of the Knight's Cross with Oak Leaves, Swords and Diamonds. Apart from my "blemish" I had no worries, for I was a good horseman.

During my interview I was asked the question, "When should a soldier complain?" to which I replied with total conviction, "Never, Herr *Leutnant!*" In retrospect I believe that that reply met all preconditions for a frictionless period as a recruit, indeed, the officers were rather comradely so far as duty permitted. Once I received a severe reprimand for going into the barracks courtyard bare-headed while still recovering from pneumonia. The NCOs, with a few important exceptions, accepted the local regime suggested by the officers. Despite this caring attitude on the part of all involved, which was well-meant, I never really felt "at home". And so it remains to this day.

The second year of my service was the worst and really depressing, but the soldier never complains. Promoted to *Oberreiter* (Cavalryman First Class) though not qualified to be squadron senior I became "maid of all work" and therefore batman to *Unteroffizier* S. who never hid from me his hostility. I lost all interest and took my revenge by loafing. After two years of general military service war broke out and my release was blocked. My transfer to the "Seniors-Horses" section, set up by the regimental adjutant von Christen, was some consolation. One horse from each squadron. Good riding training, long rides – even alone cross-country. Later I got my own back and received from von Christen my first introduction to a Panzer Mk IV!

In the opening days of the war *Unteroffizier* S. kicked me out. His complaint was my improper attitude towards him as squadron platoon leader. I was awarded a "disciplinary transfer" to the platoon of my recruiting officer, *Leutnant* Twer, whom I held in high regard. Something similar occurred later. At Stalingrad when I was accused by a corporal of cowardice, this time the soldier had to complain. Again the result was immediate transfer – but now with full honours.

Summer horseriding in Poland was what we called the opening period of the war. Riding the service mount of Rittmeister Masuhr, my squadron commander, I was guaranteed his constant observation, for even after the longest ride the hard-mouthed "Pirat" had to obey the reins impeccably. During operations in France I was summoned to the commanding officer. Von Saucken disclosed that to his regret he could not award me a well deserved Iron Cross II for my service in Poland. He made it clear how disagreeable he found it to pass on this news, but the reaction of this honourable officer did not do much to mollify me. Later the discrimination lessened. Even before Stalingrad I had received the Iron Cross I.

Over the course of time as a matter of routine I did the best I could within my grade of service. Zawadski asked me once what my problem was. When I told him he replied, "Console yourself, Dohany, with the knowledge that a good schnapps has fifty per cent!" This was no consolation but made us laugh. Finally the "ice-grey" senior private became respected under the motto "Old hands know best".

Despite my protests, I was sent on leave three days before the encirclement at Stalingrad. I had wanted not to miss the surrender of the city to German forces. When I returned I spent a day at the airstrip begging unsuccessfully – fortunately – for a flight into the city. Together with similarly excluded cases I was transferred under the leadership of a young lieutenant, von Br., to Pzr.Regt.15. Sent by Division from there to the new formation in France, to my surprise I was promoted to *Unteroffizier*. Not until later did I find out that von Br., knowing my situation, had stated that he knew of no obstruction to my being promoted. When I reported back to Division, von Knebel-Döberitz (later, as Major in the General Staff, the last commander of 24.Pzr.Div.) told me I should have refused this promotion and I ought to be court-martialled. I think he was joking.

Finally commanding a panzer, in my first action in Russia in October 1943 I was wounded. My over-nervous gunner fired without being ordered, I still had my hand on the guide-rail, the cartridge was ejected and crushed two fingers. From the main dressing station I went to the field hospital and then by goods train towards Germany. My hand was suppurating, I was in great pain and the doctor accompanying the transport had only twenty painkillers for fifteen hundred wounded. I gave up my hand for lost. We stopped on an open stretch of track alongside a hospital train heading eastwards. Empty, white-covered beds shone through the windows. Without a second's thought I changed trains. Half an hour later they operated on me and saved the hand. Through the intervention of my future father-in-law – a regimental comrade of my father – I was transferred from the reserve hospital to a field hospital in Germany where a reasonable *Ortsgruppenleiter* (a middle-ranking Nazi party official) even made it possible for me to marry.

My convalescence lasted too long. Finally I had to almost force the very friendly senior medical officer to release me. From the reserve unit I returned to the front in southern Poland and our panzers went as far as Hungary. Then we were transferred to East Prussia. Our panzers could not be transported there, and so now we were dispersed across other units.

After careful consideration it was decided that I should be a field-gendarme. I was stationed behind the crumbling frontline, pistol drawn, with orders to shoot anybody who had no recognizable reason to be pulling back. My comrades pulled back in groups but I never heard a single shot.

One night a farmer's wife, apparently alone and therefore helpless, complained that a Russian girl who worked for her was becoming rebellious. Leutnant G., in charge of the field-gendarmes, received orders to arrest her with her two children aged two and ten years. Lt.G. reported to Divisional Staff HQ when he had done this and was given orders to shoot all three at once. The task was allotted to me, and when I refused to carry it out I was threatened with court-martial. I persisted in my refusal, but today I still reproach myself bitterly for not having attempted to prevent these murders. Next morning in the village there was a great outcry when the bodies were found since reprisals by the advancing Russians were quite rightly feared. At the beginning of the 1950s I came across G. again at a soldiers' reunion. After thinking it over long and hard I decided to let it rest.

I was returned to the regiment for "unreliability" and I found my "crowd", or more accurately its remnants, further north in a camp in the forest. With my new – and last – detachment commander Major Kuls, born 1920, I sang in the soldiers' choir at Angerburg. Forced back to the steep coast of the Frischer Haff, we built rafts on Kuls' orders, and drawn by our last remaining amphibious car we crossed the Haff and reached a spit of land. Lacking experience but installed by Kuls as his driver, I was responsible for the demise of the amphibious vehicle when I filled it with diesel.

Kuls now had to make a bitter decision. He had to select thirty officers, NCOs and men from the more than one hundred members of the regiment for transfer west to the Reich. Through the long night he brooded over his decision. I shall never forget the faces of the men who learned next morning that they had to remain in East Prussia, cut off from other units: it was virtually a death sentence.

After the war Kuls came in for heavy criticism for the choices he had made from those who had got back by other means. It is understandable, but very regrettable, that as a result he became a recluse. In Schleswig-Holstein on 8 May 1945 from our last radio set we learned of the capitulation. The room fell deadly quiet. I sat at the paino and played *Deutschland über alles* softly, believing incorrectly I would never play it again. The following night I had sentry duty. Kuls came along and for a good hour we discussed whether or not Hitler had been a great man. We came to no conclusion. Then Kuls promoted me retroactively to *Wachtmeister* (sergeant) and ROB (Applicant for Reserve Officer Status) "so that I could take part in officers' meetings later!"

After my discharge from the Wehrmacht I took every means of transport, including Shanks's pony, to get south and home. I had a few difficulties in the French zone but finally got to Freiburg. By the beginning of November I was in the auditorium at Freiburg University having begun to study law.

One may say that the daily routine of these two panzer corporals passed quite unexceptionally in 12.Sq./24.Pzr.Regt. (if one ignores the difference in rank) just as it did for me. In the question of promotion to officer, however, there were substantial differences. In deciding which thirty of over one hundred members of the regiment to ship out of the East Prussian encirclement, the last commander of the detachment picked Arnim Dohany despite the National Socialist racial laws.

Chapter 7

Interlude in Northern Italy: The Eastern Front

On 17 August 1943 we loaded the panzers we had received on a train and headed for Brenner. I had become recognized as a photographer and therefore helped many of my comrades to have a photographic memento of their service. My squadron commander, who was much in favour of my passion for photography, allowed me to sit in the open on a panzer during the railway journey. Everybody else had to travel in the coaches, for on two occasions in the past panzer men had been killed, one by touching the overhead live cable, the other in collision with a tunnel entrance while standing up on a panzer.

As a result of this "distinction", in fine weather I sat in the radio operator's seat and enjoyed an airy panorama of the train journey from Magdeburg to Parma. At the destination the panzers were unloaded and on the road we received our first reprimand. The squadron commander ordered over the radio: "Column leaders to me." We knew this was not good. The reason was that the panzers had not been driven in an orderly file. In cutting tones through gritted teeth they were warned "not to move through the streets like a herd of pigs or else …". He meant punishment – or special exercises.

With our panzers – now each aligned precisely one behind the other – we drove down the Roman "Via Aemilia" via Reggio to Modena. Beyond Modena, on a wooden stake amongst a number of tactical signs, the commander of the leading tank recognized a shield with the jumping horseman insignia and the rectangular symbol for Pzr.Regt.24. This indicated the way for our regiment. The panzers left the highway and made for our future quarters, a vineyard near Bologna.

One day a small brown and white vagabond dog came running up and appeared to want to be adopted by the crew of Panzer 1241. He looked at us with such devotion and longing, and looked so much at home in and around our panzer that commander and crew decided he should be our mascot. Because of his awkward gait we named him Tapsi (=clumsy). Our new friend was always around, and once ate the contents of a frying pan left unattended on a low fire for a few minutes. On walks we used the white cord from a pistol as his lead. He stayed with us until our first action in Russia. We would like to have kept him, but in the fighting he might have been wounded or trapped, and so we gave him to the support unit. Later at Kirovograd I saw Tapsi being taken for a walk by a soldier of the catering unit. He had only little legs and his stomach brushed the snow. I was really sorry, and felt guilty about it, that this small dog had been taken by us from his sunny Italian homeland to wade through the slush of Russia. Rare feelings of guilt about a small dog!

Unteroffizier Posadowsky spoke very good Italian and was appointed interpreter. On the train journey from Magdeburg to Parma, 12.Squadron profited from his linguistic ability and people skills. Between Brenner and Trient an axle of a low loader was running hot. The Italian railways administration at that time was still our ally through the Berlin-Rome Axis – although this axle was also running hot and about to part – they refused to change the wagon. They also said they had no substitute wagon available. Thus our train was at a standstill very close to the Adige, allowing us panzer men the opportunity to bathe in fine weather in this very inviting river. Meanwhile Posadowsky kept negotiating, initially without success. He discussed the situation with the *Spiess*: "Have you any money in the squadron safe?"

"Yes, why?"

"Can you spare some for the Italian railwaymen?"

The *Spiess* agreed and the negotiations went on. A short while later a substitute wagon appeared mysteriously. The panzer was being transferred over when the driver braked too sharply on the wooden beams of the low loader floor, and one of the tracks slipped over the edge. The panzer had to move endlessly to and fro while wooden beams were piled up under the track, and finally it was got back on the wagon. I shall refer later to another example of bribery for the benefit of the squadron.

For our quarters, Posadowsky bought vegetables for the men every second day. He got to know the surrounding area very quickly and was very useful in foreign exchange transactions. The problem during this Italian sojourn was not only to have money, but to have it in Italian currency. Five-mark silver coins rated highly for exchange purposes. In these problems of money and currency my friend helped out greatly, and with the necessary small change in our pockets we could visit Italian cafés and bars.

I was invited occasionally to accompany Posadowsky on his special trips. During one such outing I was witness to the omnipotence of an officer's uniform, if worn with the necessary authoritarian demeanour, and that nothing had changed since the time of *Hauptmann* von Köpenick. A lieutenant had acquired knowledge of a goods wagon loaded with

Cinzano vermouth and bottles of champagne. Posadowsky drove our lorry and I was the bearer. He lost no time in getting the wagon opened. We had just started unloading it when a sentry appeared and ordered, "Stop! Remain where you are!" The lieutenant ignored him, at which the sentry removed the rifle from his shoulder and adopted a shooting stance. At that the lieutenant roared: "What! You dare to point your weapon at a Prussian officer?" The soldier froze with respect, so intimidated that he allowed the officer to continue with the theft without protest.

Returning from leave once, Posadowsky reported, "Uncle Friedrich is very seriously ill!" This code expressed our hope that some activity or other was about to put a quick end to Hitler and his war. Heynco also recounted how two of his cows, which had escaped from the meadow through a hedge at his second property in Upper Bavaria, were both shot dead by a passing Berliner. The man was sentenced to nine years' hard labour for his marksmanship.

At that time we were still feeling the effect of the fall of the Badoglio Government at the beginning of September 1943. The regiment had quickly occupied all the former Italian barracks from Livorno to Venice. My squadron had to take over the barracks at Pisa which involved a panzer drive over the Apennines. On the way we observed the rapid change in attitude of the Italians who had at first greeted us jubilantly, pinning on our clothing and panzers flowers and bundles of rods with the inscription *Vencere*, but now after the capitulation stood hostile and sullen by the roadside and often spat at our panzers. Hardly touched by the war, the Italians had quickly forgotten the Berlin-Rome Axis and now longed for the Americans to arrive as "liberators". We German soldiers were now their enemy and our panzers the very symbol of an enemy power in their own country which it was now their purpose to eject. Only the farmers in the Apennines gave us friendly waves and laid cigars on our panzers. This frightened us, for the cigars were so black that at first we took them for grenades.

The Italian people had meanwhile become convinced that we were running very short of vital war materials, particularly rubber. Therefore we had the phenomenon of Italians coming up to our panzers to examine the tyre tracks, retiring in astonishment upon discovering we were still rolling on rubber.

On a trip to Viareggio, Graf Posadowsky and I met two pretty Italian women on a deserted sandy beach. My friend's ability to speak Italian even aided us in our pursuit of a minor flirtation. I did not know then that within a fortnight I would experience my baptism of fire in Russia.

During our stay in Italy we familiarized ourselves completely with our panzers. The feeling of belonging grew and that the crews were welded into a close knit unit. The soldiers of 12.Squadron were by now well acquainted with each other. 12.Squadron was "our" squadron and the longer the war and the stresses of operations went on, the more we were proud to be a member of a well led and operated panzer unit. This self-identification with 24.Pzr.Regt/24.Pzr.Div. was very marked. The division was inseparably associated with the cavalry tradition, prepared by excellent training for the most diverse operations, led by first-class officers and NCOs, highly valued by the senior Army commanders and also esteemed and feared by the enemy as a special division. General von Senger und Etterlin described 24.Pzr.Div. as a unit of a special kind. It had been forged into an unalloyed whole in the furnace of war and was a sort of "Homeland" during the battles at the front. Nobody wanted to belong anywhere else even though the 24th was a "fire brigade" sent to the dangerous hotspots of each battle. That is not to say that the men did not yearn for and seize moments alone, front leave and the hours of leisure and relaxation as often as they became available.

In connection with the sacrifice of many men of 24.Pzr.Div. at Stalingrad I am inserting here an historical assessment. 24.Pzr.Div. was part of the Sixth Army destroyed at Stalingrad. Therefore a large part of the division disappeared amongst the 147,000 dead and 91,000 prisoners. Of the latter, all but five thousand starved or froze to death in Soviet captivity. Along with Hitler, senior Wehrmacht leaders also bear responsibility for the debacle not only of this battle but for the overall course of the war. While scarcely anything was heard of Keitel, head of the OKW, perhaps because his influence on the military commanders continually diminished during the war, after the death sentence at Nuremberg on Jodl, head of the Wehrmacht Command Staff, there was much discussion on his involvement. It is clear that after Stalingrad, Jodl spent almost two and a half years in the loyal execution of his duty to Hitler even though the war was lost beyond recovery. For this army leader, battles remained a good and necessary business. What would it worry a *Generaloberst* Jodl if the soldiers were expended needlessly? A large number of officers from Hitler's close environment were relieved of command eventually, why not Jodl? And why did he not walk away from the king of terror voluntarily? Thus he was the tragic, guilty counterpart to soldiers who had no desire to be at the front and fell there in a lost war. For the purposeless death of many of my conrades, respecting which I shall refer later, even a *Generaloberst* Jodl bore responsibility and in all probability guilt. The renowned historian G. Ritter calls the highly gifted Jodl a fanatical follower of Hitler. Though intelligent and an outstanding soldier, he lacked any political instinct and – above all – iron in his blood. Maltreated by Hitler, in contrast to almost all his colleagues of general's rank, he was not decorated with the Knight's Cross and yet remained as if under the influence of a narcotic, fascinated by the Führer.

As soldiers, Jodl and Keitel, who was of one mind with Jodl, came to a bitter end on the gallows. While the deserter panzer man D-- was shot by firing squad, both these men charged as major war criminals suffered the ignominy of death by the hangman's noose. In October 1991 at a lecture I asked sixty students of dentistry: "Who was Jodl?" Nobody answered. "What was *Generaloberst* Jodl at Nuremberg for?" Again no answer. Obviously in the lecture hall, and not only as an exception but at school too, something is being neglected.

Our squadron was divided into four platoons or columns. The panzers bore a unique squadron number which identified them accordingly. The leading panzer of the first column had the number 1211: 12.Squadron, 1st column, 1st panzer. My panzer bore the number 1241 which therefore meant 12.Squadron, 4th column, first panzer, a column leader. The squadron commander's panzer was known by its number 1251 and the deputy was 1252.

As a rule a *Rittmeister* (captain) or *Oberleutnant* (first lieutenant) would be squadron commander while a *Leutnant* (second lieutenant) or veteran *Wachtmeister* (sergeant) or *Oberwachtmeister* (WOII) commanded a column. When I started, a young second lieutenant was 1241 commander. Later, after we had sustained serious losses and there were insufficient officers and sergeants to go around, often a veteran corporal would command a panzer.

The radio operator in the column leader's panzer, and the one in the squadron commander's panzer, were responsible for communications from "above", i.e. between the squadron commander and the commanders of the four lead panzers. For this enlarged sphere of radio traffic two receivers were installed above my transmitter. By means of these various installations the radio operators of the squadron commander's and the column commanders' panzers were often required to operate a radio conference between themselves. In action at the front the radio traffic, complicated by call signs changed daily – e.g "Sunflower to Aster" – required much concentration.

The radio operators of the subordinate panzers had it easier because they only received incoming calls from their squadron leader, or made outgoing calls from their own commander. Because of leave or casualties there were always changes of panzer, and during my career I served in the radio operator's seat in all of them from the squadron commander's vehicle to the hindmost. I was happy to be a radio operator, wished to continue to be one, and avoided doing anything which might suggest I was officer material. In any case, I was a person who lacked all military virtues and was too young to be considered for a commission.

To a certain extent my attitude resulted from the fact that an officer would not remain with a damaged panzer of which he was commander, nor return to the rear with it. He had to stay at the front and board the nearest battleworthy panzer, while generally an NCO would replace him as commander of the damaged panzer. Twice when my panzer broke down during an attack the *Leutnant* took over another panzer in running order. Shortly afterwards both panzers were hit and the two officers killed. After incidents such as these I was even less inclined to think about officer training. I was happy to be an *Obergefreiter* with the real possibility of surviving the war.

Officer casualties with our unit were very high. I knew from our many conversations during the time we spent together in France and Italy that my friend Graf Posadowsky thought the same. In his case, however, his aim was to return to his family and properties in Silesia in order to manage them efficiently. The administrator employed in his absence was doing a very poor job. His noble birth, friends and contacts ultimately predisposed him to seek a commission. I saw him again at Sagan in 1944 when he was a second lieutenant.

At the beginning of October 1943 our divisional commander wrote a personal letter to Hitler in which he asserted: "My soldiers want to go to Russia." This had its fatal outcome. The commander was a Prussian officer who wanted to fight, and naturally the officers had the ambition to fight successfully with the panzer division and its men. What the men themselves wanted did not interest them, and nor could it in war.

Apart from the single incident with the transport platoon (1942–1943) I was never asked by an officer if I actually wanted to go to Russia, and I am sure that most soldiers would have declined. I heard later from a Staff radio operator that 24.Pzr.Div. was scheduled to be attached to a Waffen-SS unit. As a result, the divisional general, von Edelsheim, took the next aircraft to see Hitler personally and inform him "Better in Russia as the 24th Panzer Division than in Italy with an SS unit."

Finally to Russia we went. Before loading we spent a few days in the Italian spa of Montecatini waiting for the low loaders for the panzers. Whereas in earlier times the spa had been the haunt of the elegant, the wealthy and artists, now we panzer men of 12.Squadron strolled the magnificent installations and parks. I had a haircut at an Italian hairdresser's. While a young lady was providing me with the luxury of a manicure, our *Spiess* came in and saw this. At evening roll call he was able to announce with disdain that *Volksgenosse* (citizen) Böttger had had his nails done today.

I already knew what a panzer transport for several days by rail was like. After leaving Montecatini on 17 October 1943, in fine weather I sat in the radio operator's hatch of my panzer as a photo specialist: as it got colder I joined my comrades in a goods wagon or Italian passenger coach. In each goods truck a small stove was installed for which we had to collect the firewood ourselves. If the stove was correctly lit the heat close to it was intolerable but away from it, especially when the cold of Russia filtered through the cracks, it was icy cold. The transport passed through Villach and along the Wörther Lake to Vienna where a short stop was made on 19 October 1943. Then we went on to Poland via Przemysl, Lemberg, Shmerinka and on into Russia. When we stopped on an open stretch people came begging for bread at the side of the train, and here occurred the first underhand trick by a certain NCO.

Ukrainian women came alongside the train wanting to trade eggs for shaving soap. The NCO in question entered into lively negotiations with a woman. Not until the moment when the locomotive whistled and the train got under way was the exchange agreed. The woman handed him the eggs and the NCO gave her the soap. Beforehand, however, he had cut the soap in half, falsely representing that it was a complete bar. We had many opportunities previously to see the rottenness of his character. Later it became ever more obvious that this was a human swine who wore the uniform of a panzer NCO, but it would be some time before he received military justice.

The railway journey ended at Kirovograd. We drove our panzers off the low loaders. Other troop units had come with us. Because of the many soldiers who detrained here, there was lively activity in the station and the city. It was hoped in high places that the enemy's thrust westwards could be halted near Kirovograd. We went first of all to a waiting position where mail was distributed prior to the first attack. We already had a new field post number in Russia. The extraordinarily good mail service and field post even in the frontline sectors were living proof of the German talent for organisation.

Chapter 8

In the Southern Ukraine:
Defensive Fighting on the Dnieper

"From here and today a new epoch in world history is beginning, and
you can say that you were there."

Johann Wolfgang von Goethe

T he phrase above was uttered by Goethe to the young duke Karl-
August von Weimar before the cannonade at Valmy. Nourished
directly or indirectly by propaganda, many panzer men remembered
it as we rolled forwards to attack. Certain of victory we looked forward to
the coming encounters in Russia and were still convinced that our panzers
would only ever forge forwards.

Now the time had come. On 26 October 1943 we rolled. At first
12.Squadron panzers easily advanced towards Znamenka and Novaya
Praga easily, destroying forty-five Soviet tanks in three days without loss
to ourselves and taking many prisoners. Then we lost the first panzers and
the squadron suffered its first dead. The driver of the command panzer
was hit by a shell and killed. The projectile hit the ground just below the
armour skirt and bounced up through the flooring.

During the first few days of the fighting at Novaya Praga we had to
operate at night. At first it was all textbook stuff with the correct distribution
of the squadron. We spent the night in Russian farmhouses for the first
time but rarely saw the Russian civilians who withdrew into small back
rooms out of fear of the invaders. Because most attacks began in the early
morning heading east, we would often be blinded by the rising sun as we
looked forward through the periscope over the endless steppe. On one
advance we reached a great field of sunflowers. As far as the eye could see
there were sunflowers after sunflowers, close together straight and high.
With their plate-like flower heads surrounded by shining broad leaves they
formed an endless yellow carpet below a clear blue sky. "Tarry awhile, you
are so beautiful," Goethe might have said: then came the order: "Panzer,
marsch!" forbidding us to dismount and stare at the wonders of nature,
commanding us instead to trundle forwards towards the foe. The clank of
the rotating tracks swamped the sound of the breaking sunflowers being

crushed under the links of the panzer hull. It had been far too short, the glorious vista of the sunflower fields before their flattening in seconds. All that mattered now as my panzer pressed across the fields was the 24.Pzr. Div. motto: "Think forwards, look forwards, storm forwards!"

As a rule, in the evening after fighting, we had to replenish; not only our own rations in a cooking pot and coffee in a field flask, but fuel for the panzer. For this purpose a lorry carrying a large number of 20-litre petrol cans would park at the centre of the assembled panzers. According to where one's panzer happened to be relative to the lorry, the cans would have to be carried a short or long distance. The same went for the ammunition. The 7.5-cm shells were heavy to carry. If we had fired off many, then many had to be replaced. We not only had to bring up fresh MG ammunition, but also fit the rounds into a belt using a small machine. After that came cleaning the barrels of the gun and MGs.

The radio operator's MG had a telescopic sight with rubber padding attached to the barrel. To look through the instrument one had to hold the MG with the hand while propping up a headplate with the head. If the panzer was crossing uneven terrain, one would receive very unpleasant blows to the head at every jerk. This was one of the reasons why radio operators generally did not use the sight to view out, but concentrated on the radio traffic and often remained unaware of the locality through which they were passing. The commander's order to fire was addressed primarily to the gunner, who operated the gun and the turret MG. Because the radio operator's MG only fired when ordered, it was frequently never used in action. If the radio operator could not fire, he could not kill! This had the additional advantage for the radioman that he would be excused having to clean the MG barrel and thread the ammunition belt in the evening. These were further grounds for remaining a radio operator.

In action, as a rule the hatches were kept shut. The driver and commander observed the terrain through viewing slits which could be reduced in dimension by dropping a flap. The radio operator also had a lateral viewing slit but this would be blocked if additional armour plating was hung at the sides. If he wanted to see out then he had to use the sight with its very reduced field of vision. In the many training exercises the reduced vision was something to which panzer men became thoroughly accustomed, but during training one could always obtain a panoramic view by putting one's head through the main hatch. This would rarely be done in battle, and we sat in our panzer sandwiched and caged. In conversation about the pros and cons of being a panzer crewman, men from other branches of the Army would say they preferred to move with the infantry rather than sit in a panzer. It was as large as a barn door and a priority target for anti-tank guns, artillery and fighter-bombers. Without doubt that was the reality, but in the panzer I felt safer against rifle and sniper fire, MG bursts and flying metal splinters, and not every anti-tank shell hit the barn door decisively. Moreover, after an attack the panzer always withdrew to a zone of relative quiet while in winter one slept in a Russian house by a warm stove, if only on a blanket rolled out on the floor. The ever-present uneasy feeling did not come from being in a "panzer target" but was the same for all soldiers, that today a deadly shell would come flying over with your number on it.

In the midst of the fighting – in action in the forward front line – we now experienced war with all its horrors, terrible incidents which entrenched themselves deep in the mind. I can still see to this day a Russian soldier dying immediately in front of my panzer. During a long morning scrap, a couple of panzers equipped with flame throwers instead of a gun came upon Russian infantry in slightly downhill terrain. First the panzers fired a cold, black oily substance, and this was ignited about eighty metres from the enemy troops. The change from the cold jet into a great tongue of flame heightened the effect and set the earth alight. This forced the Russians to retreat up the hill where our panzers were waiting in a half-circle for their arrival. The Russians had no thought of surrender. Nimble as weasels some of them boarded our panzers from the rear with the intention of affixing limpet mines or dropping hand grenades down the hatches. Alerted by radio we fired at our own panzers with MGs to knock off the enemy soldiers and thus retrieve the situation.

Meanwhile German panzer-grenadiers had come forward. A sergeant with a machine-pistol went for the Russian soldier who would shortly die before my eyes. He had not surrendered at that point and decided on a wrestling match with the sergeant. The grenadier had great difficulty in freeing himself from the Russian's clutches, and finally the latter threw himself down before our tracks. Lying on his stomach he looked up and raised his hands a little. Whether this was a gesture of surrender was not clear. My commander ordered the gunner to shoot the Russian with the MG. He fired at once but at this short distance hit the soldier between the upper arm and body because of the error in alignment between the telescopic sight and the MG barrel, and he kept firing at the same spot. The Russian, still on his stomach, remained looking at the turret with staring eyes and slightly raised hands, his feet upright on the toe caps. It was some time before his boots drooped which signified his death. I had to watch this intolerably protracted act of his dying through my sight. When my commander ordered me to fire too, to my relief the Russian soldier was clearly dead, and once again I had escaped having to kill.

That same evening our panzers attacked down a slope towards a village. At first the advance was unopposed. The order came to commence MG fire at the village during our approach even though there was no sign of the enemy. We used tracer to improve our accuracy and I found the rapid fire released by my trigger intoxicating. Inside the village all was tranquil and the order came by radio to halt. Scarcely had we ground to a standstill than a heavy artillery bombardment began. Shells exploded around us throwing up clods of earth, chunks of cottage and metal splinters. We had no orders to advance or manouevre to some safer position. I was terribly afraid. I felt that the end was near. I put my hands together and prayed: "Dear God, help, dear God, may we get out of this! End the bombardment or let us make a run for it. I am still so young, I have not yet begun to live!"

After an intolerably long time the voice of the squadron commander came through the headphones: "Panzer *marsch*!" Off we surged through the continuous shelling and left the village. Later I experienced similar bombardments while in battle under heavy artillery and anti-tank fire in which my panzer was hit repeatedly, but by then I was much more philosophical. One got used to it gradually and came to terms with the danger and the constant fear of death. To a certain extent it was "the main purpose of being here". Although this was only a prelude to the real frontline action, in the next few days the grave, pallid, exhausted faces of raw young soldiers, almost still children, had made the transition from youths to grown men.

The fighting lasted mostly from 0330 hrs till nightfall. We kept German time: what the Russian clock said it was did not interest us. After six days at the front I wore the Panzer Badge in Silver (this badge, worn at the left breast pocket, was awarded to panzer crews after the third attack), and I wore it with pride. Now at least the difference between veteran soldiers with front experience and the "young upstart" was partially removed. Privately I thought that something was still missing – the Iron Cross! This created a dilemma: on the one hand there was caution, not to become embroiled in the fighting and so survive, on the other to seek a decoration which distinguished the soldier, put him on a par with veteran and well-proven front comrades, and gave him recognition as a frontline soldier when on leave in the Homeland. And above all, in the eyes of the common people and to the uniformed Party functionaries, the golden pheasants of the Reich, he was seen as a blameless German privileged by war.

One evening a panzer got stuck in a bog. A second one came to assist and suffered the same misadventure. Now they both needed help. Several panzers including 1241 attempted to pull the casualties free using tow ropes and acting under radioed instructions. Repeated attempts failed. Next the inevitable happened: the motor of 1241 became overheated and broke down. Now 1241 also needed to be pulled out. A rope was attached to the towing lug. One jerk and the entire fixture broke away. Eventually our panzer was dragged to the side of a house in the nearby village and parked. The other two panzers still required assistance.

Over the next few days the squadron headed towards Krivoi Rog without problems, and behind the fighting troops went the tow-truck and repair team. Help for our non-operational panzer was now out of reach and 1241 had to be towed eighty kilometres back to Kirovograd for repair. The crew – naturally an NCO had taken over as commander from our lieutenant – billeted themselves in a small house in the village. It was built of white loam with a straw thatch typical of Ukraine dwellings. Inside it we slept on simple beds or blankets on the floor near the stove. Because of the damaged engine we could take no further part in operations and had to wait for a tow. We slept well and next day shot at pigeons on the roof with our P38s. This frightened off the pigeons. After a brief wait the pigeons returned. We kept shooting, but never hit a single one. Lucky pigeons!

In the afternoon we strolled through the little Ukrainian village where we met Waffen-SS men from a unit stationed nearby. They invited us to eat with them. Whilst we Wehrmacht soldiers were permanently hungry and during the recent bouts of fighting 12.Squadron had had to live on dehydrated vegetables, the SS unit served us roast beef and potatoes the first day. The second day everybody had half a roast duck, followed by a large piece of pork; for dinner huge hard-smoked sausages, liver and so on, also cheese, butter and honey. Along with Army bread came crispbread, cigarettes and cognac. The fat of the land. Now I saw with my own eyes the outstanding provisions enjoyed by the SS, and the privileges and preferential treatment enjoyed by the Waffen-SS over the Wehrmacht, and not only in the rations but also in weapons and equipment.

We were in the rear, far from the fighting, had plenty of sleep and now these banquets! We should have been satisfied with that but soon we experienced very briefly, and all the more enduring a memory for that, another side to this dreadful war. After the crew of 1241 had had their eight hours' sleep on the fourth day, we wandered through the village towards the SS unit. Suddenly we came across a human figure hanging from the branch of a tree. It was a man, head downwards, secured by one ankle, wearing the Jewish star sewn on his jacket and quite dead. Curiosity turned to shock. It was a gruesome spectacle, I had never seen a dead body strung up before. Distraught, I was in no mood to take a photo. As we all stood there looking, a soldier of the SS unit came by. He confirmed what we had suspected: his unit had hung up this Jew. The SS-man explained it was a reprisal for his having taken part in partisan activities. In silence we returned to our quarters. We were not only paralyzed mentally, but also feared to speak of it amongst ourselves. Still young and relatively inexperienced, the war had begun to blunt us. I hoped never to see the same thing again. In shame, my camera stayed in the pocket of my uniform.[1]

---

1. On 28 October 1943, elements of 24.Pzr.Div. were relieved by reconnaissance units from the *SS-Totenkopf* Division.

Chapter 9

Behind the Lines at Kirovograd

After the tow which I mentioned in the preceding chapter, the damaged 1241 arrived at Kirovograd in November 1943 and the crew occupied a very pretty little house. It had parquet flooring on which we unrolled our blankets to sleep. Kirovograd was a town to the rear of the front where a few things were on offer for the troops.

The lady of the house was a very friendly Russian who spoke some German. When her husband was taken off – it was said he was forced to be an armaments worker – she was naturally very sad, but incomprehensibly she wept more bitterly for us when we left almost six weeks later.

In Kirovograd was a soldiers' hostel with a bookshop and other diversions such as table-tennis. We were soon friendly with the nurses, and went to the hostel almost every day. On 8 December 1943 the nurses evacuated the hostel and loaded their bags on a train, which signalled to everybody that Kirovograd was to be abandoned. Besides visits to the hostel, we went to a cinema frequently. Although there were three of them, they did not have room for the great numbers of soldiers behind the lines needful of entertainment. One had to be at the front of the queue very early to be sure of a seat, unless a great throng of soldiers stampeded, a frightening event requiring a field-gendarme to fire his pistol into the air to regain some form of control.

On 1 December 1943 the *Wochenschau* newsreel showed panzers from my squadron. It gave me a bad conscience: my comrades in the thick of the fighting and here the crew of 1241 lazed uncomplainingly in the rear. In contrast to the three soldiers' cinemas, the front-bookshop never came under pressure. There were volumes of knowledge for educational purposes, e.g. preparation for the *Abitur*, but the bookshop was usually empty. Soldiers did not lust for knowledge. Behind the front they had more basic desires. The best soldier in the world behind the lines could occasionally be excused a call at a brothel. A condom was required to be worn. After sex a "curative soldier from the medical corps" would paint the soldier's member with a silver nitrate solution and then issue a "certificate of health".

Kirovograd was not only a large town behind the lines, but was awash with thousands of German soldiers. One could take the panzer for a day's excursion along the front line and never see a German soldier. This inequality between fighting troops actually fighting and the huge mass of troops resting at Kirovograd was unmistakeable and further strengthened the strong doubts about a German victory. General Schörner had recognized the problem and attempted in his own way to chase soldiers out of the rear to reinforce the fighting troops. That he lacked the means and ultimately failed, while the numbers of dead and wounded increased enormously, is known and should be known. That his court-martial sentences have been compared to those handed down by the judges of the People's Court has distinguished him as an especially brutal general.

Oberst Rudel was at Kirovograd with his squadron of Stukas, which had its own dance orchestra and entertained troops with hit music and shows. I had a very unpleasant encounter with Rudel. The soldiers' radio station "Gustav" at Kirovograd was holding an evening of entertainment which I wanted to attend. I had no ticket and waited at the door. The hall was full but with goodwill it should have been possible for a couple of soldiers to find a spot to stand. During a discussion with a field-gendarme acting as bouncer, Rudel, who naturally had a front-row seat, came up to me and snapped, "If you don't shut up at once I'll have you thrown into a cell!" Lock me up for wanting a spot at a variety performance? I considered the intervention of Hitler's No.1 aviator extremely arrogant, Interested only in himself and showing his power, even enjoying it, he had no feelings for the simple soldier.

Later I went again to the soldiers' variety. Radio station "Gustav" left at about the same time as did the nurses from the Kirovograd hostel – a further indication of the approach of Soviet forces. The field post office shut its doors on 9 December 1943 and a couple of days later our damaged panzers were pushed aboard low-loader wagons before the train steamed westwards for the Reich. Before proceeding with my narrative, I must now go back a little and devote a few chapters to the "war career" of that NCO who in so many situations proved what a miserable pig he was.

Chapter 10

The Swine in a Corporal's Uniform

"First comes the meal, but even then not yet the moral."
(After Berthold Brecht)

Whilst waiting for our defunct panzer to be towed out from the Ukraine village, the replacement commander for 1241 arrived. This was the corporal of the shaving soap trick whom I shall grace henceforth with the name "The Swine".

In the little Ukrainian house where we had our billet only a young wife remained. The male inhabitants had either run off or been taken to Germany for forced labour. This woman had a piglet, probably the private property of her husband, a collective farmer. Besides the house, her clothes and cooking utensils, this porker was the only thing she owned, or at least, we could see nothing else by way of belongings.

The tracked towing vehicle arrived and our panzer was coupled up to it. When we were about to leave, the Swine gave the order to seize the piglet. This was a low blow. Over the last few days we had eaten excellent fare with the SS and far more than we needed. "Why do we need this small pig?" I asked, and implored the Swine to let the woman keep it: "You cannot take away from this woman the last of her belongings," but he told me from his position of authority, "The pig comes with us!" I could not disobey the order, and in any case the animal had already been stowed beyond reach aboard the towing locomotive. The piglet was then slaughtered in Kirovograd and the crew of 1241 all dined on it.

I may lay myself bare to accusations of hypocrisy when I admit I did not refuse my portion, but I was within legal bounds. The piglet had been "requisitioned", slaughtered and roasted, and if everybody else ate it, why should I be the exception? War was as simple as that, but the whole business irritated me. After the meal the Swine ordered me to chop wood, which was unnecessary, for we had plenty. Always and in every situation he had to show off his rank.

The Swine was a very good organizer. While we were chopping wood he came up in a new Opel Olympia car with a full tank. The vehicle shone in a livery of newly-sprayed field-grey, and he introduced it as "My car". His car? How could a Wehrmacht saloon become *his* car? A few days later he turned up in "his car" with about ten full canisters of petrol as luggage and ordered me to get in. The drive took us to a sunflower oil factory a few kilometres away. When we got there he gave me an order, and only then did I realize why he had brought me along: I was his bearer, a task beneath him – "I give the orders". As instructed I carried the canisters into the factory and brought out a corresponding number to the car. This episode would have been clear proof of his special talent for organization and well worth a mention had its purpose been to barter more rations for the men. But no, he had organized the sunflower oil exclusively for his own private trading later in Germany.

In another bitter incident involving the Swine, our panzer was loaded with other damaged panzers aboard a goods train for repair in Germany. While waiting to leave, the Swine had "his car" put on a low loader with another panzer. There was no room in the car for a passenger, for it was crammed with food of all kinds, some of the sunflower canisters were on the floor and smoked sausages hung in rows from the interior roof. At first this car and its provisions did not particularly interest us. At the "change of the watch" during a stop on the journey, my gunner and I kept an eye on the low loader bearing this car, the damaged panzer and the other wagons generally. Still on watch, a passing Russian told us in broken German: "Tomorrow Russians here" and asked us for clothing. We let him have a bloodstained military greatcoat, which probably came from a military hospital.

The train then resumed its journey westwards and we dreamed of the Homeland. The crew of 1241 was travelling in a goods truck. At another halt the order reached us that only the Swine was to continue with the transport, the rest of the 1241 crew was to change trains and return to the east, the new destination being the frontline in the area of Nikopol, to where 24.Pzr.Div. had advanced in the meantime. With long faces because we were no longer going to Germany, we requested the Swine, who obviously had the luck of the devil in the travel arrangements department, to at least let us have something to eat from his "car of sausages". His answer was, "You get nothing" and he stated this in the same tone as when he had told me, "The pig comes with us!" The sausages dangled in inviting fashion behind the windscreen and before our noses and we begged "Give us just one sausage." He waved us away with the coarse retort, "No, you get nothing, not one sausage." We were enraged. Instead of going home it was the front again and not a single sausage!

In disbelief my gunner and I exchanged looks. "This Swine, this filthy Swine" was my reaction. The other members of 1241 felt the same way. Should we give this blackguard a good hiding such as the one of which Erich Maria Remarque had written so unforgettably in *All Quiet on the*

Western Front, or should we smash the windows of his car with our pistols? By doing the latter we would be damaging Army property, however, and before the eyes of the Station Officer, who was standing on the platform together with the Wehrmacht hierarchy from corporals upwards. Thus in my helplessness I found myself in the same situation as the sentry who at the Italian railway yard had aimed his rifle at the lieutenant and achieved nothing.

Aboard the transport to Nikopol we saw Christmas approaching and we were far from home. On 21 December 1943 we associated with a Red Cross nurse who had a modest Yule tree in her room on the station and tried to work up some Christmas spirit, then the journey continued and next day we rejoined 12.Squadron and got into our panzers.

The final chapter involving the Swine was completed elsewhere. Facing the prospect of more fighting, we almost forget this loathsome corporal. It was required of us to report everything which had occurred in general during our enforced absence from the squadron and especially in Kirovograd. The rumours about the Swine thus came to the ears of the squadron commander. One day the crew of 1241 was ordered to report to him. Under questioning it was made clear to us that the theft of petrol, a commodity essential to the war effort, was considered a serious offence. Once he got back to Germany, the Swine had managed to work himself into the reserve unit at Sagan. Some time later our *Spiess* went there to attend a court-martial. On his return he told us that the Swine had been found guilty and reduced to the basic rank of *Schütze*. Compared to the sentences reportedly handed out by General Schörner at Nikopol and Marasati, and the death sentence given to panzer man D--, one has to remark that in the end the Swine did indeed have the luck of the devil.

Chapter 11

On the Defensive in the Nikopol Bridgehead

As soon as we got to Nikopol station we saw what kind of military overlord was in charge of the bridgehead. Whereas stations in the Reich had their walls decorated exclusively with Nazi slogans such as "All wheels must roll for victory" or "Pssst, the enemy is listening", here in the station were posted the sentences handed down by the brutal and authoritarian General Schörner. For example, an officer had been sentenced to death for transporting mattresses in a lorry, these not being essential war materials: an *Obergefreiter* had been condemned to death for not heading for the nearest fighting unit (identifiable by the sounds of battle) after having been cut off from his own unit: a corporal who contracted a venereal disease was given twenty years, and so on.

Many such stories circulated about Schörner, all of which spoke of his ruthlessness and harshness. He was said to have promoted or demoted drivers for good or bad driving respectively. A captain came riding up with his valet. Schörner sent the valet to the infantry. The captain protested, "Excuse me, Herr General, he is my valet." Schörner told him, "Then you can go to the infantry with him."

In action, panzer men carried their service pistol attached to a cord around the neck or through the shoulder strap. Outside the panzer it was worn in the holster on the belt. Mostly the weapon would be unloaded, for otherwise it was not without its dangers, and especially when being cleaned there had been repeated injuries. Because the pistol barrel must not be allowed to rust under any circumstances, we usually wrapped it in an oil-soaked rag. When Schörner came across a 12.Squadron soldier one day he ordered him, "Fire at once into the air!" After opening the holster the soldier had to unwrap the pistol from the oily rag. Then he had to load it. Schörner gave him 21 days arrest, then asked him, "Which unit?"

"24th Panzer Division!"

"I forgive you the punishment!" Examples of the power of a warlord with absolute power of command.

From Nikopol we drove our panzers to the frontline and crossed the

Dnieper and its tributaries across sturdy wooden bridges erected by the engineers. Our division was involved in very heavy fighting in the Nikopol bridgehead. Because I had the *Abitur*, the *Spiess* assumed I could write a quality essay, and I was sent to assist a sergeant of our squadron to compose a Christmas Day battle report for a newspaper. I took up the pencil and wrote thus:

The panzer-cavalry men of 12.Sq./24.Pzr.Div. will never forget destroying twenty-eight enemy tanks without loss to themselves in scarcely an hour during a very heavy day of attacks. It was a cold winter's day: thick fog hid the frontline. 12.Squadron led by Oberleutnant Wenzel had the task of occupying a waiting position behind the frontline. The enemy bombarded the German positions with artillery for ninety minutes: this was the usual sign of new activity from them.

Every 12.Squadron panzer commander waited for the radio message to roll. Repeatedly they wiped the optics used to monitor the terrain. It was a time of great tension. Slowly the fog dispersed to reveal a steely-blue sky of a winter day in the East. The artillery fire gradually fell away: in the headphones they heard the voice of the squadron commander: "Enemy tanks, 11 o'clock, squadron roll!"

At once the panzers set off for an artificial feature where the grenadiers crouched in their foxholes. Suddenly we saw thirty enemy tanks heading on a diagonal approach course towards the grenadiers' positions. At the order "Fire at will"· everybody knew how grave the situation had become. "Don't just fire, hit!" With a crack and a whizz our panzer shells found their mark, but the enemy tanks and SP-guns kept rolling towards our grenadiers' positions.

The grenadiers, who knew they were safe under the protection of our panzers, allowed the Russian tanks to pass over them and then engaged the enemy infantry at the rear. *Wachtmeister* Blonski's column had halted the main enemy assault and a destroyed a third of the enemy tanks. The squadron commander recognized that the right flank of the 12th was no longer fully engaging the enemy, and therefore ordered *Wachtmeister* A to leave the right flank and extend and reinforce the left flank. Now the enemy attack was brought to a standstill by the combined shellfire of the 12th. Twenty-five of the thirty enemy tanks were hit, the rest fled. During the subsequent pursuit, a further three were destroyed.

Wachtmeister A. saw several enemy tanks halted on the left flank. A couple of crew members examined them and established that two T-34s were still battleworthy. On this particular day, 12.Squadron inflicted a severe blow against a much more numerous enemy and over a period of twenty-two days of engagement raised their tally to tank kills to 132.

R. Hinze wrote of this day: "At the boundary between 258 Inf.Div. and 3. Gebirgs (Mountain)-Div., enemy tanks broke through and caused a temporary crisis in this sector. Elements of 24.Pzr.Div. counter-attacked at once and neutralized the danger by destroying twenty-seven enemy tanks."

Oberstleutnant H. H. von Christen, 1a officer (chief operations staff officer) of the division, told me of an intercepted Russian radio message on 25 December 1943: "The Germans are now going to get drunk because for them it is Christmas."

Now we had to prepare for the operations at Nikopol during the fierce Russian winter with its frequent icy winds. Our supplementary uniforms for the period consisted of padded camouflage jackets with hoods. They were reversible, white or grey-green in colour. Although they gave some protection against the cold, we were often frozen to the core. During pauses in the fighting I would tell my driver to "keep the motor running and revolutions up", then take off my leather boots – my feet were size 46 (English size 11) and they did not have this size in fur boots – and put my feet in the exhaust chamber to warm them. We heated the interior of the panzer with a very efficient petrol blow lamp equipped with an air pump which helped produce a very powerful flame.

During engagements, nobody would ever be reprimanded over a dirty shirt collar or uniform. Nobody cared that one's apparel, from the cap to the trousers, above all in the combination chosen, did not comply with dress regulations. As my various photographs confirm, the soldier decided for himself if he would wear the green or white side of the reversible jacket, the black jacket with or without pullover, or the fatigue jacket; and black trousers or camouflage ones, laced shoes or field boots, side cap or panzer cap; grey, grey or black shirt and, for me personally, a pistol or camera. At Nikopol when my squadron drove up for photographs on the order of the squadron commander, I took out my camera from my pistol holster. None of the many higher ranks who watched me at work, not even the strict WOII, asked where my pistol was. Only when you presented yourself for home leave did the uniform have to be reasonably correct.

As a result of the numerous field operations we carried out, the breakdowns to our vulnerable Panzer Mk IVs piled up, as compared to the T-34. Replacement parts were ever more frequently demanded: High Command failed to provide the necessary quantities. Our *Spiess* reflected

My father's military pass from Saxony
(König August).

A painting of *Unteroffizier* Paul
Böttger, gunner with 1.Horse
Battery / 1.Feldartillerie.Regt 12.

"In the Time of Iron". Medal for donations of gold for the Army, 1916.

The Order of the Grand Duchy of Baden awarded to my mother for service as a nurse during the First World War.

Reverse face: "I gave gold to the forces, I accept iron for honour".

Cross of Honour without swords for auxiliary personnel (instituted in 1933 by Hindenburg).

Schoolboy French proved useful for flirting with this salesgirl in a Brionne seed shop.

Occupied Paris; German soldiers at the Arc de Triomphe (1943) and at the tomb of the Unknown Soldier "fallen for France".

A stroll through Magdeburg in 1943: it seems no different for peacetime except for the lack of motor vehicles. This is the Ulrich Kirche in Otto von Guericke-Strasse.

Heynco Graf Posadowsky-Wehner wearing on the ring finger of his right hand an engagement ring with a diamond and two small sapphires. Later, after he was wounded, a female Soviet officer at a field hospital stole it together with his cigarette case.

Passing a field-gendarme in the streets of Bologna on the way to artillery practice in the mountains. The gun is a German light field howitzer 18/40.

Keeping contact with home was the most important off-duty activity: the author writing a letter with dipper pen and blue ink.

Our small adopted dog Tapsi in pert stance on the turret of 1241.

Rear view of 1252, support panzer for the squadron commander: the man behind the tank wears the Afrika Korps uniform with shorts and laced boots.

A Bologna crossroads with no signpost leaves a panzer crew uncertain.

A civilian Fiat car painted with white stripes (blackout precautions!) heads past the squadron on the road from Bologna to Bazzano.

on what could be done to overcome this spare parts calamity. He recalled the centuries-old, proven technique of greasing wheels, and sent one man technically qualified in radio communications with five helpers to the Army Supplies Office at Magdeburg. They did not go empty-handed to request spare parts, for the *Spiess* gave them as much cognac and champagne as they could carry, and which had been brought originally by the rearward support from France and Italy. Thus the baggage of the "Kommando" consisted almost entirely of alcoholic beverages. When the Kommando returned, they brought not only three railway truckloads of spare parts, but some new panzers as well.

Proudly the *Spiess* reported at regiment the acquisition of spare parts and new panzers. The answer he received from the commander was that of the prophet: "*Oberwachtmeister* S., we have known each other long enough. I tell you now: if what you say is true, that we can no longer obtain panzers from OKW, but can purchase them with schnapps, then the war is lost!"

My panzer – now 1244 – was hit several times in the fighting at Nikopol and rendered unmanoeuvrable. One shell hit the slanting front-armour without effect. Another time during an air attack on 15 January 1944 by a "sewing machine", a Polikarpov Po 2, in which small bombs were dropped, many panzer-grenadiers close to our panzer were wounded and we received a hit on the barrel of our gun. This gave the impression of being precisely at the centre of an explosion: every nook and cranny cracked and rattled, sparks illuminated the interior of the panzer with a garish light. The actual effect on the gun was slight: a small dent was the only damage, but a new gun had to be fitted and that required a short stay at the rear. We could breathe again, for when 1244 was in the workshop, the crew could sleep in, and I had time to write home. I told my mother about the most recent front activity: "For a couple of days the Russian artillery fired at us like crazy. We were glad to be sitting in a panzer where one is safe from shell splinters."

I was told that since 12 December 1943 I had not received any post. The one constant factor in all the horror was the Homeland. Without mail from home, something to which one could hold firm was missing. I was depressed, and five days later on 22 January 1944, I wrote home mentioning that I had been waiting for mail since 12 December 1943 (and therefore over Christmas), which must have conveyed the impression of how upset I was.

The Nikopol bridgehead was hotly defended by our division. We acted as a fire brigade which had to intervene when things flared up so that the Russians were denied a breakthrough. Suddenly on 23 January 1944 came orders to leave the bridgehead. The unit crossed the Dnieper over a bridge built by the engineers and loaded its panzers on rail trucks for a two-day journey to Uman. The sudden departure from Nikopol was made with the intention of forcing a breach in an encirclement by the Soviets at Cherkassy.[1] We loaded the panzers quickly, the Russians hot on our heels.

---

1. Stahlberg, former orderly officer to *Generalfeldmarschall* Manstein, Commander-in-Chief, Army Group South, reported of this event that after their successful offensive over the Dnieper, west of Cherkassy the Soviets had succeeded in bottling up 42nd and 1.Army Corps. After a situation conference with Hitler on 28 January 1944, von Manstein sent the following radio message to Army Group South: "I.Panzer Army: proceed with attack III Pzr.Corps and XXXXVI Pzr.Corps with all available means in order that once enemy forces there have been removed, III.Pzr.Corps and SS-Leibstandarte *Adolf Hitler* can head to the north east and so engage enemy forces attacking VII Army Corps from the rear. VII Army Corps to hold situation, if possible maintaining current position with Corps detachment D until 24.Pzr.Div. moving up, or the forces released by 8.Army, can engage those elements of the enemy which have broken through."

Chapter 12

With Damaged Panzer on the Russian Highway

On 3 February 1944 we de-trained. Driving along the street a singing noise began at one side of the panzer. The transmission had gone. We remained immobilized for two days at the roadside until a passing panzer gave us a tow to the nearest village, near Tishkova, where we parked between two houses. Since we had no food we broke open the panzer emergency rations. These rations were supposed to last three days and consisted of a case containing ham, dehydrated vegetables, lard, tinned bread, Scho-ka-koila (chocolate with caffeine) and a 100-gram cube of 60 per cent compressed coffee beans with 40% sugar, plus a drink to take if on the march. For the soldier a fabulous assortment.

Because food always played a dominant role throughout the war, I remember well a number of stories which did the rounds amongst soldiers concerning *Generalfeldmarschall* von Manstein's diet: "At Manstein's they only have butter, but when the *Führer* visits, they serve margarine." This was confirmed in a certain sense by Major G. Naumann, liaison officer on von Manstein's Staff who reported on the food in this HQ: "A colonel asked a major, "Have you got a man here who can go down to the officers' mess?"

"But of course."

"Have him bring up a bottle of champagne, God knows I feel like it."

For lunch in the Commander-in-Chief's mess, orderlies served meals the equal to any five-star restaurant, beginning with soup followed by main course and dessert. Then came cognac in silver holders and a choice of tobacco wares. Of particular note was the gift of several cases of oysters on ice sent by *Feldmarschall* Rundstedt to Manstein from France. Manstein thanked him by return with a small cask of caviar and cognac. Since it involved a flight of "only" 3500 kilometres (per G. Naumann), it was sent by plane.

After resting near Tishkova we set off to look for a supply point. The commander and crew of 1244 hitch-hiked to the nearest locality for the purpose, Novo Archangelsk. At a Wehrmacht care centre, such as was on hand in every large town, we received our road rations. To our delight we found a soldiers' hostel there with nurses. To a soldier's eye these girls were always pretty, attractive and alluring, and erotic impulses simmered. Meetings were much too brief, however, and sex without love was unthinkable for the young, inexperienced soldier.

Our billet was twenty kilometres away from this town and relatively far, but there was always heavy traffic on the Soviet-built highway and so we hitch-hiked to the soldiers' hostel regularly by car or lorry or even as pillion passengers on motor-cycles, returning in the evening.

Almost four weeks passed. At the porch to the soldiers' hostel I photographed the Commander-in-Chief, 8.Army, General Wöhler, who enjoyed frequent stays there. He asked us panzer men for our unit: "24. Panzer Division, Herr General!"

"A very able, strong force," was his reaction, and conversed with us in the most friendly manner. What a change from Schörner! He would have sent us to the infantry at once. I have to say I was surprised to see a Commanding General in a soldiers' hostel at such a time, the crisis which had developed in and behind the 8.Army frontline being the worst in the Army Group South sector. Until then I had supposed that a Commanding General would always be in the battle zone in such a grave situation. (After the war General Wöhler was indicted as a major war criminal at Nuremberg and sentenced to eight years' imprisonment for war crimes on two of the four major counts.)

Meanwhile it had begun to snow again. Our panzer was blanketed, as was a pile of used straw (we were sleeping on the floor again) which we had thrown out in front of the house the day before. I could not find my camera which I always wore around my neck and only took off while I slept. The whole crew searched for it without success. We asked three Russians who lived in a side room. Nothing! A short while later a Russian came to the door holding the camera. Without being asked he had gone outside to look for it and found it when rummaging through the straw under the snow. Overjoyed I gave him a couple of packs of tobacco for his kindness.

Isolated from our unit, on 22 February 1944 a Wehrmacht report reached us. 24.Panzer Division had received a special mention for its proven performance. In what way "proven"? Acting on an idiotic order, 24.Panzer had sallied forth to destroy three Russian tanks and then returned to the starting point. They bogged down in the mud and we also lost rear support and other vehicles. Thus from my own experience – as happened later in action in Poland – I saw how wide was the gap between reality and such bulletins.

At the beginning of March 1944 the nurses left the Novo Archanglesk soldiers' hostel and so we knew that a retreat was in the offing. The mud-covered highway soon filled with vehicles driving back, together with masses of soldiers and auxiliary troops all plodding westwards.

Our commander sent me off with two crewmen while he and the driver remained behind for the purpose of destroying 1244. I mention the name of this silent man, who was an unusually good and humane NCO: *Wachtmeister* Rudi Lotze, a baker by trade from Lauenburg. For us there was never a better commander, not for heroism at the front, but because he knew that the crew was composed of young men, almost still children and not experienced men, and handled them accordingly. He was an upright man, and for us he was a hero. He always thought of us first, then of the panzer, since that was or could be our fate, and finally of himself. In action he commanded the panzer cautiously and with reserve, but also courageously and with determination when the occasion demanded it. After an attack he was the first around when fuel or ammunition or food had to be fetched, and the last to leave. Whenever possible, he would send off the young men of his crew to relax and sleep in the billet.

Without any song and dance he introduced a very useful invention (made by himself?) on our panzer, which saved us much onerous work. It involved a weak point of the caterpillar track. The tracks were held together by almost two hundred bolts which fitted between the track links. On the outer side they were secured by S-shaped cotter pins. In motion these pins tended to break off, and now the bolt would push inwards until it broke off, struck by the undercarriage. The remaining bolts would then slip out and the track could fall apart, rendering the panzer non-operational. At every stop the first thing the crew had to do was examine the tracks. If any S-shaped pins were missing, new ones had to be inserted in the angled bolt-holes and the projecting ends of the pins hammered until bent. Lotze had a metal plate welded at an angle on the rear fuselage. If a bolt moved inwards, it hit the slanting sheet which pushed it back outwards. The track could now run securely even without the pins. Later I saw this installation on a Russian T-34. This excellent sergeant fell during the heavy fighting involving 24.Panzer Division at Jassy after his panzer was hit by heavy anti-tank shells, He could have been back behind the lines, for he had been wounded in the face by shell splinters when I spoke to him on a reverse slope during a brief pause in the fighting. He made light of his wounds and went forward toward the white ruins of Stanka castle where he was hit and died in the panzer turret. On this last run he had no longer been my commander. My own panzer was commanded by a lieutenant. It suffered engine failure. He changed panzers and was killed soon after. Meanwhile we waited half a day behind the lines for a replacement engine.

Back to our departure from the unbattleworthy 1244. With great difficulty we made our way along the congested main highway, first on foot and then hitch-hiking, to a front command post at Pervomaysk on the Bug river. From there we were sent to Odessa by train. It was absolutely packed and we stood the whole 54 hours. I had seen German troops retreating often enough and looking at the Bug I wondered why at least some kind of expanded defensive line had not been set up along this wide river, if not a kind of Westwall. German troops had fought outstandingly in numerous bloody defensive battles, but they still kept on pulling back.

On 19 March 1944 the rest of the 1244 crew joined us at Odessa. Up to this point, as far as I know, my division and regiment had always seized the initiative and held its ground in all previous actions. I had always gone forward with 24.Pzr.Regt. Now one saw only too clearly that we were going back and only back. For the first time I was fleeing, and this was a demoralizing realization. Depressed, I described in a letter to my mother that although I was a soldier with an especially strong division, I had been to a certain extent pulling back for a few days. Now even I doubted in victory, as had my mother always.

At Güldendorf near Odessa, a former *Volksdeutsch* village whose inhabitants had been forced to leave, we met our 12.Squadron comrades on 21 March 1944. The squadron itself was rather dissolute and without panzers and had a bleak look. The roll was called. The last panzers had been lost around Nikopol or had had to be destroyed. In this waiting period – waiting for what we had no idea, would it be for rifles so that we could join the infantry (quote from a letter: "That would be the worst shit") or panzers again? – the officers remembered their cavalry tradition and rode around on horses. Three men were to be sent on leave, and I was one of them. It turned out to be another long journey.

Chapter 13

Journeying on Leave

With the leave pass in my pocket and a certificate from my squadron commander that as a soldier coming from the front I was entitled to special rations, namely the heavy labourer's supplement and two eggs per week, I went with two comrades to Odessa airfield where activity was hectic. Aircraft landed daily with supplies and returned to Germany mainly with the wounded. After a long wait a large four-engined Ju90 flew in. As soon as it landed the ground staff went to work at once, bringing out bright wooden crates containing replacement engines from the fuselage. We joined a group of walking wounded, and with them we three leave-takers could board and fly to Mühldorf near Munich. There was an intermediate stop at Bucharest where we passed first through lice-control. Trousers down, and after an inspection by a medical corps man I was "passed" despite one or two small lodgers in my vest. From Munich we took the train to Freiburg, and after twenty-three months I had home leave at last.

At home my mother coddled me. Now I could sleep my fill, free of orders or the sounds of battle. The best the kitchen had to offer – helped along by saved-up food and ration coupons – appeared on my plate. Cared-for and not ordered about I felt a little of freedom: this was how life would be if one did not have to return to the front. The fear of death was thrust aside temporarily to be replaced by the fear of being watched. A leader of the women's organisation with long pointed ears and 100 per cent loyal to the Party lived in our house. One had to learn to whisper and listen to enemy radio broadcasts with the greatest possible caution.

I visited the cinema frequently and enjoyed listening to records again. The days passed quickly, but as my leave approached its end the days became overshadowed by my imminent return to the front. I doubted that I would come home from the war healthy and in one piece and became especially depressed at the thought that this was perhaps my last experience of my family. After a tearful departure I went alone to the station. My mother and I preferred to avoid saying our goodbyes on a railway platform, providing the spectacle of a sobbing mother and her weeping soldier son while strangers looked on, or a Party official with a superior expression.

The journey back took me through Munich on the first day and to Vienna on the second where a connection was supposed to be waiting for Rumania. By the fifth day when it had still failed to materialize, and the transport officer confirmed that no train was yet available, the men stormed into the city of Vienna with a loud roar.

We finally left for Bucharest on 27 April 1944. The stages of this rail journey took us through Klausenburg to cross the Carpathian mountains, four steam locomotives being necessary, two at the front and two in the centre of the train – and into Ploesti, but the train kept going. I discovered the reason at the next halt on an open stretch of track. Lying in a meadow I watched an air raid on this important oilfield town by wave after wave of bombers. Black clouds of smoke still hung over Ploesti as the train resumed its journey to Bucharest. We arrived there on 5 May 1944 and reported to a front organisational office. These posts were to be found on all large stations. The soldier would discover from it where his unit was stationed and how he should get there. Next day I went by passenger train – just like in peacetime – back to Ploesti for Bacau. I sat with farmers, civilians and Rumanian soldiers in a fourth-class compartment. The journey through a countryside without war was ghastly because of the stink of garlic. The train dawdled from station to station, calling at Mizil, Buzau, Rimnicu, Sarat, Focsani…. At every stop I got off and stretched out in the nearest meadow. At Marasesti on 6 May I stood once more before a scene I recognized: all the walls of the little station were tapestried with new posters bearing decrees in the old and well-known tenor of General Schörner. Now I knew where I was. In the long stops at stations along this line I saw everywhere such pitifully clothed Rumanian people that the warning signs, "Soldiers, death sentence for looting" fitted Schörner but less the realities. What was there here to plunder? Some Rumanians were even wearing grey Wehrmacht socks with white rings, or parts of uniforms which they had obviously obtained in exchange or barter from German soldiers.

After an unbelievably long journey from Germany which overall took twenty-five days, the train got to Adjut, Bacau and Roman, from where I hitch-hiked a ride on a lorry and reached my unit of 12 May 1944. To my astonishment there was an airmail letter from my mother waiting for me, which she had posted after I left!

Chapter 14

The Fighting at Jassy

"In the midst of life we are in death."
Luther, after the old hymn
Media vita in morte sumus

During my leave the division had received new panzers. 12.Squadron had been deployed to a forward zone between Pruth and Jassy after a Russian advance north of Jassy. At supply I found a repaired panzer and climbed in. Now began again those terrible days for German and Russian alike when the Grim Reaper rode along with us. After such a long time together we panzer men naturally knew each other very well: one was more friendly with one, less with another. On the evening of my first attack in this war zone I heard of the death of a radio operator colleague with whom I had spent a lot of time. A shell penetrated the interior of the panzer, killing both the driver and radio operator. Thus fell *Unteroffizier* Lorenz. After that came blow after blow, just like the story of the Ten Little Nigger Boys, set in brutal reality.

Next evening six or seven panzer men sat around a table. Twenty-four hours later five of them were dead, four from one crew alone. One morning seventeen panzers were operational and by the evening only six of twenty-two. From this one could estimate "when one's time would come".

On many evenings soldiers would play the card game "17 and 4" in their quarters. Because we were paid in Kreditgeld (occupation money not valid in the Reich and forbidden for transactions with the local population) it was difficult to know what to do with it, and so betting in Kreditgeld reached enormous proportions. One particular evening there was more than 10,000 RM in Kreditgeld notes on the table. A very young soldier only a few days with the squadron won the pot with the right card and stuffed the notes into his pockets. It was the last time he won in his life. Next day his panzer was hit. When they carried his body back, the Kreditgeld notes were sticking out of his bulging pockets.

The area around Jassy was a malarial region and we had to take Atebrint tablets every day as a prophylactic. During the fighting in the zone itself at times the temperature would soar to intolerable levels. We sweated profusely and were always thirsty. The sun heated the panzer plating like a stove and most definitely one could fry an egg on it. Unfortunately we had no eggs, but were plagued instead by a fearsome thirst. The two field flasks filled with coffee (without milk) in the mornings were soon empty, as was a captured Italian jerrican which could hold ten litres of water. By midday the question was: "Is there anything else we can drink?" A 20-litre petrol can, washed out with water and then filled with more water was kept in the panzer during hot weather as our last reserve. In case of need we resorted to this water, hot and flavoured with petrol.

Of course, on days of action the fighting troops received better rations, including bean coffee and a small pack with Scho-ka-kola to sweeten it. Cigarettes (made by the firm Reemtsma of Austria, etc) were very important, and were distributed with every issue of rations. Almost every soldier smoked, and not a few were so addicted to nicotine that not only did they smoke during breaks but puffed away throughout an attack: they needed a kind of nicotine intoxication to be "brave".

One of the following evenings our squadron commander notified us of a major offensive for the next day (Operation Sonya, 30 May 1944); "First the artillery will fire, then the Luftwaffe will come with Me 109s and Stukas (Rudel's squadron), preparing the terrain for our panzer attack and to support us. Then the 12th will go forward, and nothing will stop us until we reach the Pruth."

We had settled down on our blankets for the night alongside our panzers when suddenly an inferno of fire awoke us from deep sleep. Unknown to us, a multiple rocket projector had been positioned close alongside our panzer. With a great flash of fire and a dreadful long-drawn out detonation it discharged its rockets through the early hours. Was this a good or bad sign? At four in the morning – as promised – the artillery bombardment began, and the German warplanes came to our support. We were positioned on a reverse slope with the grenadiers, who waited in their trenches. Once they had gone forward to the advanced trenches the attack began with the order "Panzers, *marsch!*"

We had gone only a little way when wire wrapped around the tracks of our panzer and snarled up so badly that we could not run a straight course. We had to get out to free the tracks of the wire and lost valuable time waiting for the wire-cutters. Because the terrain was still mined there could be no talk of an easy advance. Opposite us was a slight rise. The Russians could fire at us from an elevated position, and they fired at us "from every buttonhole". We shot back, of course, but never saw a Russian, and had to aim at their muzzle flashes. Our advance stalled, and we remained stuck in an unfavourable position. Then the Russian shells began to fall all around us.

My panzer got two shell-hits on a running wheel below the undercarriage.

Luckily the Russian aim was not good. Eighty metres away to our flank a panzer of our squadron had been hit and immobilized. A crewman lay on it, half naked, his uniform completely tattered, thigh bleeding, hit by an explosive shell. He was obviously in terrible pain. The back of his leg had spread open like a cauliflower by the explosive effect of this murderous shell. Without asking my commander's permission, I jumped down from our panzer to fetch this wounded comrade. Together with a crewman from the disabled panzer I carried the wounded man over to our panzer and laid him on a blanket on the plating. Despite the padding he felt the heat of the plating and cried out. But where else could we put him? In soaring temperatures our panzer headed at full speed for the back slopes. Alerted by radio, our surgeon came forward immediately in his specially equipped panzer and after examining the casualty gave him no chance of survival. At the same moment another panzer arrived back also carrying a severely wounded man, picked off by an enemy whom we never saw once in this skirmish. There was a large hole in his back, a shell had torn away a large chunk of flesh of two hands' width. The endless agony of death on the battlefield was etched in his green-yellow pallid face. He had been a very rowdy young man, perhaps even a hooligan, but now he only whimpered, "Mother, help, mother help me." The surgeon looked him over and announced that he too would be dead in a short while.

In the hour of their dying they lacked comfort. From where should this come? At first we panzer soldiers had spoken words of comfort and reassurance as we stood around the dying man and the surgeon. Maybe they eased for him the anxiety and fear of death. No chaplain was present. Whether there was one in our unit I have no idea. The veterans recalled a religious service at Gomel in 1941 which made a big impression, but during all my time at the front I never saw a clergyman.

That my panzer received more damage to the engine during the fast run back, and that the commander changed panzers and was killed shortly thereafter I have already mentioned. This was also the day when Rudi Lotze left for the front towards the ruins of the white Stanka castle, where he fell. Whenever I remember these events, the horror of this terrible war resurfaces before my eyes. For my Samaritan deed without orders, next morning I received the immediate award of the Iron Cross, Second Class.

Before another attack on 2 June 1944 I heard a call for the surgeon to attend our former squadron commander, who had meanwhile been promoted to regimental adjutant. He had been sitting on a panzer reading a letter he had just received from his wife when a shell exploded nearby. A splinter passed through an eye into the brain and thus he died a hero's death. Just before he had been awarded the Ehrenblatt clasp to the Iron Cross, a newly-created intermediate award below the Knight's Cross which he had certainly deserved. At the award ceremony the regimental commander had pronounced the well-known formula: "You receive this decoration also for the services of the unit commanded by you" which meant all 12.Squadron. After this the squadron assembled for the last time around this outstanding soldier for a small celebration in an orchard.

His strict but good panzer training has already been mentioned. In action he was a first-class commander who led the panzers of his squadron very circumspectly: "1232 take care, Russian anti-tank gun at two o'clock. 1224 move over further left, terrain is better there." Regarding the course of this extraordinarily tiring attack I described my role the following morning in a letter to my mother: "It is half past five and we have just left the battlefield. From yesterday at 0100 until now I sat in the panzer the whole day and night. I was command radio operator. Because of the heavy radio traffic to the squadron commander and the individual column leaders the greatest concentration was required, and this practically without a pause. The weather was not so hot as yesterday, but because we had to drive all the time with the hatch closed the radio operator's seat alongside the big motor assembly was baking, and I had to wear the headphones the whole time. Never once did I have a bite to eat and we drank the water reserve in the canister dry. Now we are off to the repair team to recharge the batteries."

Another event in my military "career" took place a little later on 30 June 1944. In a quiet period at a squadron celebration, the men settled down on the grass. Before them stood an *Unteroffizier*, a grenadier and I. Every man had a cooking pot filled with 38% Nordhäuser schnapps. We three were first given a bulb of garlic in which a hole had been drilled and filled with salt. This had to be eaten at once and washed down with schnapps from a brimming small beer glass. This ceremony marked the act of promotion whereby the *Unteroffizier* became a *Wachtmeister* while my friend and myself were made up to *Unteroffizier*. The celebration followed. Only schnapps was available and everybody drank it as though it were water. Over the next two days the heavens circled round and round ceaselessly. Thirty years later I still cannot beat the smell of schnapps, let alone drink it.

Before I was carried off to my quarters in a drunken stupor I do recall the return from leave of a private from the medics who announced his engagement "under special circumstances". They filled him up with alcohol so quickly that he collapsed like a felled tree. A couple of grenadiers organized a white sheet, covered him with it and lit six candles around its edges. This was his symbolical burial. Fun and reality were close bed partners.

From an Order of the Day shortly after 20 July 1944 we learned of the failed assassination attempt on Hitler's life. Perhaps it might have ended the war. In the tension between duty and conscience, for a few their hatred for the regime which always had us firmly in its grip now came to the forefront. Because the attempt had failed and we found ourselves in the midst of the hurly-burly of war, the bitter situation of the simple soldier quickly showed itself. The war situation was the decisive factor and indifference to the political situation was soon restored. Scarcely one of my comrades ever entertained the idea that an illegal regime had sent us into this war, and most considered that they were defending the Fatherland and not the Hitler regime. As G. Benn wrote, the way we looked at it was: "I have taken the fate of my generation upon myself without asking if it be good or evil, or if it brings with it glory or annihilation."

The major change to affect us was the instruction that with immediate effect the Hitler salute replaced the normal military salute in which the right hand touched the peak of the cap. Now we had to do what the Waffen-SS had always done. This alignment with the uniformed Waffen-SS – even if only a partial aspect – annoyed me greatly, for I was proud of the Prussian salute I had been taught and which generations of soldiers before me had used.

After the heavy fighting previously mentioned our squadron moved to the outskirts of Jassy. The main highway passed close by and it was possible to take public transport almost to the frontline. This did not appeal, and so we went back into Jassy by panzer and stopped at a soldiers' hostel. Exhausted and filthy we sprang down from the panzer and downed several beers. In the pauses between the fighting we used to watch farmers tending their fields unimpressed by the war. During this short break *Oberwachtmeister* (WOII) Blonski arrived, a man who wore the Iron Cross I and was proven in many battles. He was due to attend the War Academy shortly to become an officer and asked me if I would help him with History. Thus the *Abiturient* who because of his education had so often been condemned as an inferior soldier during his time as a recruit, was now freed from daily formal duties to be a history tutor. As an ensign in his current rank after his course at Panzer Troop School 1 at Krampnitz, Blonski received a very good certificate. This document remarked on his interest in history but also that he held solid soldierly National Socialist views.

After the death of the former squadron commander I was ordered to photograph the graves of our fallen squadron members buried in the "hero's cemetery" at Jassy. A painter came to put the inscription on the simple wooden crosses. He had a long list of names. After writing them neatly on the bar of the crosses they would be inserted into the ground at the head of the grave. Flowers were then laid and now I photographed them. Of all my many exposures taken during the war only two rolls were lost. I regret very much that they were these.

After this photographic exercise I went as an instructor to a Rumanian unit. Over eight days, which included a training drive, with two comrades from my division I instructed Rumanian soldiers in panzer radio procedure. At that time they were fighting on the German side, but were not that far from defecting.

Allied bombers spent ninety minutes hammering our rear section at Jassy. As the bombs fell endlessly we sheltered cursing in a slit trench. During this training course I lost contact with my unit which had been loaded aboard a train to defend East Prussia, the Homeland of 24.Pzr.Div. They got no farther than Poland where the fighting was more intense. A little later I followed after 12.Squadron. I knew they would soon be in action again, but the sense of belonging to my panzer squadron outweighed my regret at heaving to leave the Rumanian unit behind the lines.

Chapter 15

Awards and Decorations:
Pro Virtute et Merito

The Iron Cross developed during the war to become one of the most important rewards for one's involvement in battlefield endeavour. Simple soldier and officer both wanted to wear a decoration so that in the relationship between superiors and subordinates, and men of equal rank too, one might claim to be the better soldier, even a privileged man. The sergeant without the Iron Cross I lacked an important decoration as against the sergeant who had it. In my squadron there was a corporal, later promoted to sergeant, who had the Iron Cross I as commander of a panzer and also wore the Silver Wound-Badge for five wounds. He used to say quite freely, but he meant it, that he was hoping for one more "light" wound so that he could wear the Gold Wound-Badge and everybody would think, "This is a hero". In this connection I refer the reader to J. C. Fest's question as to what was striking about Hitler in 1933: he had the Iron Cross I, a high award for a mere private soldier.[1]

It is interesting to note that the institution and renewal of the Iron Cross from 1813, 1870 and 1914 was a Prussian decoration while that of 1939 was an order of the German Reich. With the 1939 renewal the difference between the Iron Cross as an award for personal bravery and for services at command level fell away. Previously the distinction had been identified by different medal ribbons for fighting and non-fighting men respectively. Accordingly one could not tell from the Knight's Cross of the Iron Cross of the Second World War whether the wearer had been awarded it for bravery or for being a successful commander.

In most cases it was only a man's rank which indicated the reason for the award. A private soldier for example could hardly be decorated for successful command nor a general or senior officer – with the exception of some Luftwaffe officers – for service at the front involving a weapon.

---

1. Hitler finished the Great War in the rank of *Obergefreiter*, senior private. Though commonly referred to as a corporal in the literature, he was never an NCO. There was no such rank as lance-corporal in the German Army: the lowest ranking NCO was a full corporal, *Unteroffizier*. Tr.

Thus no private or NCO won the Knight's Cross of the Iron Cross with Oak Leaves and Swords.

A certain hierarchy of awards was recognizable throughout. The NCO received the Iron Cross II for taking part in a certain number of engagements in the field, the sergeants and officers of junior rank the Iron Cross I, and from squadron commander upwards after successful actions the Ehrenblatt clasp, the German Cross in Gold or even the Knight's Cross. Later the Oak Leaves would follow and for a general who had commanded an army for a long period, the Swords. Bravery was also measured by the Silver or Gold Close-Combat Clasp (fifty and seventy-five engagements respectively) and the Panzer Combat Badge for fifty and seventy-five engagements respectively, rightly considered the highest awards for bravery.

An order might be awarded as a parting gift. When Hitler summoned *Generalfeldmarschall* von Manstein, Commander-in-Chief Army Group South, to the Berghof, he informed him that the period of attacks was over and he was therefore transferring Manstein's command to *Feldmarschall* Model. Then he awarded Manstein the Oak Leaves and Swords to his Knight's Cross, which he would then wear constantly, to a certain extent his parting gift.

Generalfeldmarschall Keitel stated that Hitler used to insult and humiliate him, and then honoured him with the Knight's Cross and field-marshal's baton. He never felt comfortable with this decoration for he had done nothing by way of personal bravery or leadership to deserve it.

Many ordinary soldiers received awards for bravery. Von Langenn-Steinkeller from our division knew the highs and lows of the campaigns in France and Russia as a cavalryman, and later when it was reformed as a panzer division he was always in the most forward frontline as column commander, squadron commander and regimental commander, happy to accept responsibility and make decisions. After he won the Iron Cross I and II in the French campaign, in Russia he received the German Cross in Gold and as regimental commander the Knight's Cross. As he had never been away from the frontline he also had the Infantry Assault Badge and the Close Combat Clasp, and the Gold Wound-Badge for the injuries he sustained.

An order might be earned without any particular act of bravery. If a sharp-eyed panzer commander spotted an enemy and his first-class gunner then hit the target, this met the conditions for an award. The infantryman or grenadier, however, had far fewer opportunities, although no matter what the weather or terrain he might come face to face with the enemy.

In my squadron, *Wachtmeister* Ott had the "luck" to be on the edge of a forest glade when suddenly some Soviet T-34s passed by. He destroyed eight of them. His reward was the Ehrenblatt Clasp (mentioned in the

A Panzer Mk IV Variant G without armour skirts. Additional track links are fitted at the front for extra protection. Left of the chassis number is the radio operator's MG 34. The headlights on the mud guards have slit covers.

Lt. S. addressing the squadron. Taken during gunnery training at Bologna. In the background are the sergeants of 12.Squadron.

Pzr.Regt. 24 on cross-country manoeuvres: SP-gun 943 of 9 Squadron/24 Pzr.Regt. camouflaged with netting in Italy.

The radio operator's side of the Panzer IV: MG mount alongside the chassis number and the driver's open hatch cover, above are the main gun and turret MG.

A show of force: Pzr.Regt 24 in the streets of Bologna (1943). The commander in the turret wears the Afrika Korps uniform

Consequences of the capitulation of the Badoglio Government: 12 Squadron leaves Bologna for Florence-Prato-Pisa-Livorno via the Apennine mountains.

On the lookout for Badoglio soldiers: 12 Sq./Pzr.Regt 24 heads for the Apennines.

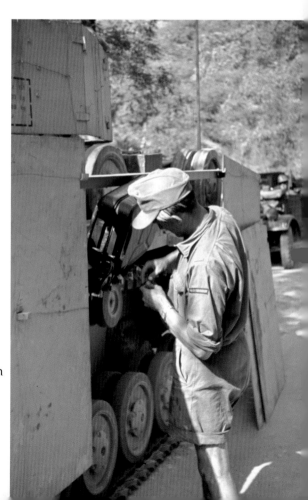

In order to refuel a Panzer IV, two sections of the armour skirt are removed and a 20-litre canister secured between the track and the metal frame. The fuel runs through a funnel into the tank. At the same time the NCO (rank insignia is the green stripe on the shirtsleeve of the Afrika Korps uniform) refills his cigarette lighter.

The war is still far away: the promenade at Viareggio.

Off duty on a quiet beach at Viareggio, a last chance for some flirting before seeing action on the Russian Front.

Unteroffizier Graf Posadowski on the beach at Viareggio in 1943. A good view of the pistol holster.

The radio operator with headphones and throat microphone looks out of the hatch of a Panzer Mk IV. The hatch cover is folded forward in front of him. Additional side armour hides the *Balkenkreuz*. In the background the leather-upholstered cover for the commander's cupola can be seen.

In France the panzer man (1943) wears the black uniform with gold piping, epaulettes, collar patches and cap.

The last picture in Russia (1944) in the billet near Novo Archangelsk. The author wears a Fascist black shirt captured in Italy and black trousers.

In the midst of war: as-yet undamaged Freiburg with the Martinstor, Below the Reich eagle is inscribed one of the greatest unfulfilled promises of the century: *sub umbra alarum tuarum protege nos* ("protects us under the shadow of his wings").

Freiburg Oberlinden with its lemon tree; the typical roadside "benches" protected by frames because of the blackout. Left, the "Goldener Bär", the inn sign of the oldest tavern in Germany. In the background is the cathedral.

Army Ehrenblatt despatches, 15 December 1944) to himself, while the gunner received the Iron Cross I and was promoted to *Unteroffizier*. Ott went on to win the Knight's Cross shortly before the war ended.

A particularly long and colourful career was enjoyed by *Unteroffizier* (later *Wachtmeister*) Willy Bachor of my squadron. He was born on 4 May 1921 at Kellbassen/East Prussia, the ninth child of the family. After elementary school and a farming course he volunteered for the Wehrmacht. On 5 December 1939 at Angerburg/East Prussia he joined 6.Sq./Reiter-Regt.2/1.East Prussian Cavalry Div. Bachor was known as a daredevil. He rode a horse in the French and Russian campaigns. From 1942 he was a panzer commander until Stalingrad, where he was seriously wounded. After the reformation of 24.Pzr.Div. in France he was attached to 12.Sq./24. Pzr.Regt. During a number of attacks I could observe his accuracy from my neighbouring panzer. It was always said, "Bachor sees better with one eye than most panzer men with two." He always hit the target quicker than anybody else. We valued him highly as a kind of life insurance during attacks. He was awarded the Iron Cross I and II, the Gold Wound-Badge, the Ostmedaille, the Panzer Combat Badge-50 for his many engagements, the German Cross in Gold and in the final resistance to the Soviets at the end of the war in his Homeland East Prussia, the Knight's Cross.

An especially exciting drama for the Knight's Cross is described by G. Koschorrek in his book *Vergiss' die Zeit der Domen nicht* in the passage *Vom Ritterkreuz zum schlichten Holzkreuz* ("From the Knight's Cross to the simple Wooden Cross"). Soldier Gustav of Panzer-Grenadier Regt.21/24. Pzr.Div. was in charge of two MGs. With a colleague he had suddenly lost touch with his platoon. The colleague explained: "When I came out of the wood with my gunner II, I saw three T-34s on the edge of the wood whose crews had got out and were engaged in a lively discussion with an officer. We set up both MGs behind the trees, then Gustav and I opened fire. Two fell dead at once and we took the rest prisoner. We established that the tanks were protecting the Soviet flank and they even had an artillery spotter to direct their fire. What happened next was a real occasion for rejoicing. From the edge of the wood we could literally pour everything we had into the enemy trenches. As a result our fighting units, which had become bogged down, got back to their feet and the regiment finished off the Russian trenches with only light losses to ourselves. Yes – and that is all there is to report. For the capture of the three tanks and shooting up the trenches, Gustav received the Knight's Cross and I got the Iron Cross I.

"Great stuff," the listener may say, "but really it was just good luck, because Gustav lost contact, wasn't it?"

"Obviously, but nobody asked what happened next."

"So where is Gustav now?"

"No idea. He was summoned to the regimental commander on account of the Knight's Cross, since when nobody has seen him. It is said he was promoted to *Unteroffizier* and had to take a course, but nobody knows anything more."

Later the colleague reported that Gustav had gone to a "suicide squad" and had fallen, together with his men, storming an enemy position on 11 November 1944. "Dear Friend! Your fame with the Knight's Cross lasted only a few months until remorseless Fate decreed that the proud Knight's Cross be converted into a simple wooden cross. You left behind only the memory of a good and highly valued comrade who became a hero unintentionally and therefore had to die sooner than those who sent you to be slaughtered." Thus G. Koschorrek's account.

My squadron commander *Rittmeister* Hupe – decorated with the Iron Cross I on 28 October 1941 – received the Ehrenblatt Clasp (a golden swastika fitted as a clasp on the Iron Cross II ribbon) for his careful leadership of 12.Squadron which during the operations near Nova Praga destroyed forty-five enemy tanks. I think he should have had the Knight's Cross. My later squadron commander *Oberleutnant* Wenzel received the Knight's Cross for twenty-seven enemy tanks destroyed by the squadron on one day at the Nikopol bridgehead, Wenzel also fell shortly after receiving the award.

After the fierce fighting at Jassy, on 23 October 1944 my divisional commander, now General of a Panzerkorps, Reichsfreiherr Maximilian von Edelsheim, received the Oak Leaves and Swords to the Knight's Cross, the 105th soldier of the German Wehrmacht to be so honoured. War correspondent Kurt Scheit wrote: "This high award was made to *Generalleutnant* Reichsfreiherr von Edelsheim for his outstanding service in the struggle for this area of Russia, after his name became almost a byword for the German will to resist during the winter of 1943 and spring of 1944. At that time *Generalleutnant* Reichsfreiherr von Edelstein headed a division with which he had served in the field in 1939, of which he had commanded a squadron and then the regiment; a panzer division whose name had a special ring not only for our glorious units, but also for the enemy's ears as well."

But back to *Obergefreiter* Böttger. How were things with me? First I received, as already mentioned, the Silver Panzer-Combat Badge after my sixth engagement. I was very proud of this award which looked very eye-catching on the black material of the panzer uniform and announced that this panzer man had already fought at the front and proved himself as a soldier and a man.

During our enforced stay outside the encirclement at Cherkassy, Russian reconnaissance aircraft and so-called Polikarpov "sewing machines" used to fly over our billet in the small village alongside a Russian house without spotting our parked panzer. One day I was sitting in the gunner's position and aimed the cannon at a Russian aircraft circling our village enticingly. "He should be quite easy to shoot down," I thought. I glanced at the loader. "Put an explosive shell in the breach." During my reflections on how to sight the weapon to allow for the three dimensions in which the aircraft flew, my commander shouted, "Arnim! Leave it! If you fire, you'll have all their aircraft over our billet!" I was already dreaming of my Iron Cross for shooting down the aircraft. The intervention of my wise commander brought me back to reality just at the right moment.

Three months later there followed the heavy fighting my squadron had to endure at Jassy in 1944. On the morning of 3 June after endless engagements our panzers spent a whole day and night in the rear area. We refuelled, carried ammunition and fetched rations from the kitchen lorry. Then along came a sergeant with whom I had long been on familiar terms. I greeted him with a cheerful remark but snapped to attention when he suddenly began: "In the name of the *Führer* I award you..." and knotted the black-white-red medal ribbon of the Iron Cross II into the button-hole of my dungarees, which we wore in place of the black uniform on hot days. "Mein Gott, they award you the Iron Cross along with your rations," I thought, but was happy nonetheless. The Iron Cross II had been awarded to me partly for soldierly virtue in the best sense, not for a certain number of Russian tanks destroyed, but for my act as a "good Samaritan" by jumping out of the panzer and crossing territory under enemy fire to save a wounded comrade from a neighbouring panzer. I received the certificate later.

Chapter 16

A Mysterious Camp

A long train ride took me through Hungary, Czechoslovakia and a short distance to Debica in Poland. In the search for my unit I suddenly found myself outside a camp whose name even today I still do not know but was, I assume, a concentration camp, presumably a small annexe of the Auschwitz complex. I saw about two hundred persons, identified as Jews by the star they wore, being led by guards away from the camp and across the fields. The camp itself appeared to have been evacuated, for the buildings were empty, there were no prisoners to be seen inside and the gates were locked.

Even though people find it hard to believe; my comrades and I knew nothing of the systematic annihilation of the Jews. As a student in Freiburg I had seen the Jewish star on the chest of many inhabitants. I had seen the sign in the swimming baths: "Entry forbidden to Jews". Equally I did not fail to notice the broken windows of Jewish businesses in Freiburg after Kristallnacht, nor the SA men who stood outside them. I remember being particularly shocked by the smashed windows of the Lichtenstein men's outfitters, where my father often shopped. I was sympathetic towards these Jewish retailers and at the same time feared the SA men, who unleashed a sensation of absolute and omnipotent power. Ideas that the Jews were guilty and deserved everything they got, and that what the SA did was justified, were completely alien to me.

On the morning of 9 November 1938 following Kristallnacht, from our classroom at the Berthold College I saw the synagogue burning. In class the boys yelled and shouted, especially when one of them showed a prayer book which had been thrown out of the synagogue for him to pick up. Then the teacher came back, Party badge in his lapel, and shouted for silence. We quietened down at once and applied ourselves to matters of Greek grammar. When we heard another explosion, some of the boys laughed and were reprimanded immediately by the teacher, but we hardly gave it much thought afterwards.

I remember also that our classmate Fraenkel, daughter of a highly respected University professor who had emigrated to England with his family,[1] had simply gone. I had occupied the seat in front of her for two

1. When he returned to Berlin after the war, he was brutally killed during a "68-er" uprising.

years. I reacted with surprise to a classmate's information and confirmed for myself that the cheerful, chubby-cheeked, freckled girl with glasses would not be back. I knew of the discrimination against Jews, one heard of concentration camps, but of what went on there, not to mention the planned murder of Jews, we knew nothing.

Had not the comedian Weissferdl stated on radio that he had just been released from a concentration camp, and he didn't want to tell any new jokes for fear of being sent back? And had we not heard of the tennis player Gottfried von Cramm, sent to a concentration camp for homosexuality, to work there as a prisoner? Thus we thought that a concentration camp was a special kind of prison. The Jews themselves knew nothing about the fate in store for them. Rather we thought that the Jews would be relocated in the East. The newspapers said that the resettlement area in the East was ready and the Reich Government wanted to create a broad basis of viable farms in firm ownership. And had I not myself as a soldier worked as a forced labourer gathering potatoes with Jews?

Some time ago a young American asked me if I knew anything about the Holocaust as a soldier. I denied this. In response to my "No", he asked somewhat dubiously what I would have done if I *had* known. I replied, "Nothing". There was not the least thing I could have done, and not only because the ordinary soldier lacked the means but also because my comrades and I had enough worry about in our own situation in order to survive. How intensive was the struggle to survive was to prove a few days later.

The curious but unsuspecting eyes of the soldier saw in this camp nothing out of the ordinary, at least nothing which would have interested a photographer. I took so many photos in the war, so why not there? Because I knew nothing and found nothing! There were water tanks for air raid purposes and the few things visible through the windows reminded me of the delousing installation at Brest-Litovsk. The only thing of interest I saw was an avant-garde, large 8-cylinder Type 87 limousine made by the Czech automobile manufacturer Tatra bearing an SS number plate and standing outside a house. Had I known the terrible truth, then I should have photographed the camp out of curiosity and not only the SS motor car.

Chapter 17

Seriously Wounded: *Virtute in bello*

Once I had found 12.Squadron I reported to the mobile office set up near a half-tracked lorry and got back into a panzer. The driver greeted me with a joke about my promotion in Russia. After an action on 3 August 1944, 12. Squadron still possessed two panzers. These were parked with some other armoured vehicles on even ground. The expanse of territory reminded me of the endless fields of the Ukraine, although without the sunflowers. Through the night crewmen did two-hours turn about on watch in the turret while the rest of the crew slept in their seats. At dawn on 4 August 1944 I could hardly keep my eyes open when my turn came.

"Panzer *marsch*!" The familiar order came for a new attack. It would be my last. We were to free the highway at Meilec with our two panzers and seven SP-guns divided into two squadrons (a complete squadron was officially twenty-two panzers). Our panzer drove along a stretch of road between Debica and Meilec. The hatches were shut and it was too much of a problem to peer out for long through the MG sight. I saw some fields briefly, lined with poplars, and a row of trees near a highway, and then came the order to fire. Very heavy artillery fire from close by was so loud told us at once that we were in a serious predicament. I still hand my hand on my MG when the first shell hit the turret with a deafening crash and explosion.

The driver put the gears into reverse and attempted to back out of the danger zone through fast zig-zags, but our panzer could never be fast enough in this situation. The Russian anti-tank guns scored hit after hit, and once we had sustained a number of hits on the turret we lost manouvrability. Once the motor fell silent there was a sudden peace which in reality did not exist. I looked towards the driver's side and was taken aback to see that his seat was empty, and the hatch above it open. "You must get out" was my next thought. I tried to open my own hatch but it had jammed immovably. The radio operator's hatch, like the driver's, had been thoughtfully designed for the case where it could not be opened normally. It was a hinged lid whose hinges were not attached to the armour casing but held in place by bolts retained by a metal rail and a screw. Although I got the rail and screw free (which should have enabled me to push the lid aside) the hatch was jammed in place by the shell hits and could not be budged. Behind me the gloomy interior was illuminated by a lustrous fire. For a moment I thought I must be burnt to death, and deadly fear overcame me.

Planting my feet against the hatch, my back on my seat, I pushed upwards with all my strength. "It must finally give," I thought. It refused to yield. There was only one possibility left open to me – "You have to get out through the burning turret!" At this moment the gun was at twelve o'clock, that is to say, it was pointing straight ahead. This was the biggest stroke of luck in my life. At eleven o'clock the huge metal frame of the breech would have blocked my way to the turret. Because I could not have got over to the driver's side because of the radio installations in the way I would have been trapped and burnt to death there.

As I jumped through the fire in the interior I felt its tremendous heat on my face, hands and arms. On hot days we used to roll up our shirt sleeves, and so the sleeves of my fatigues jacket slipped down as I reached for the loader's hatch, baring my lower arms. This leap across the burning turret saved my life at the expense of first and second-degree burns to my hands and face in doing so.

I had my head out of the hatch in the open air when I felt myself being jerked back by the neck as though the panzer did not want to let me go. I was still connected to my seat by the long cables of the earphones and throat microphone. I made a dive to get free of the hatch and landed alongside the panzer like a sack of potatoes, tearing off the earphones and microphone cable. I had lost my cap but worse my goggles. As usual I was wearing my camera around my neck instead of my service pistol, and so the camera survived while the pistol remained in my emergency pack inside the panzer; I had forgotten the pack in my haste to bale out even though I could have grabbed it as I went. I had often gone over in my mind what actions I would take if I had to abandon the panzer in an emergency, but the reality of having to escape from a damaged and fiercely burning panzer during a battle was something else.

I glanced at my watch and saw it was 0600. I crawled to the impressions left by the panzer tracks in the earth and followed them away from the panzer with the aim of putting distance between myself and the inferno. I was unarmed, but even a pistol instead of a camera would have changed nothing. Alone on the battlefield, no comrades in sight, oppressed by the sense of being left in the lurch, the panzer radioman without a panzer, frightened and with his strength ebbing, I looked for an escape route.

After a short distance my conscience told me, "You are an NCO and should make sure your comrades are safe". So I crawled back to the fiercely burning panzer. It stood between two other armoured vehicles, both in the same state. No German soldiers were to be seen. Looking at these three wrecked machines it was clear to me that this was the end, this was my Waterloo. Now I lay just as wounded and beaten on the battlefield as those defeated Frenchmen after Napoleon's last battle, and like countless soldiers in all the battles of history before and after them. Where was my Napoleon? Probably in some safe bunker somewhere playing war games on a map while the combat soldier lay abandoned on the battlefield as the battle raged on.

Despite my injuries I thought immediately of taking a photo of the battle, but my arms and hands were so painful that I could not open the camera case. The shells stored inside the panzer began to explode, and then finally the panzer blew up. I pressed my head to the earth and crawled away quickly. At this time I did not know that my commander, *Oberwachtmeister* Assmann, had lost his life. A hit had taken both his legs, leaving him with no chance. The other crewmen were nowhere to be seen, and I searched for them in vain.

At first I crawled along the panzer tracks and across a potato field, then across a cornfield mown flat. I had been taught in the barracks that when under fire in a field without protection one should advance by bunny-hops, sprinting and then throwing oneself down. So I did so and found that this was quite a different proposition in a mowed field than on the barrack square. MG fire hissed around me. The morning sky was grey as the artillery battle beat out its infernal rhythm, and before me lay a choice of a potato field or mowed cornfield at right angles to the roadway.

Near the roadway was the row of trees I had noticed on my last look through the MG periscope in the panzer. I jumped and crawled, jumped and crawled until I reached the end of my strength. In this phase of exhaustion I was suddenly indifferent to it all and simply stood up. I would go for the road running upright in the open as if the war had passed me by. My fear had drained away. I had put some distance between myself and the enemy, sufficient that his MG fire was out of range. A deep ditch ran towards the road, in it I was able to make more progress with better protection. Even so the situation was not without its dangers, and after I had covered a considerable distance in the ditch I came across a German anti-tank position whose soldiers shouted from behind their gun: "Get under cover, there's a Russian anti-tank gun over there!" Having already escaped the worst the enemy could fire at me, this well-intentioned warning did not impress me in the least.

I saw a panzer of the 24th coming up. It was our medical panzer with the survivors of my crew sitting on it. They greeted me: "Hey, Armin, so you got out. We thought you were fried!" How quickly they forgot everybody else once the panzer started burning! And I had crawled back to it to check there was nobody left there! Naturally my colleagues were overjoyed that I had survived. It had not crossed the mind of any of them that I might be trapped inside needing help as perhaps the crews of the other two panzers had needed help! One last greeting: "You're still alive then, I can hardly believe it!" Yes, I was alive, badly burned and still wearing a singed fatigue jacket, but now all that mattered was life, survival.

The OKW bulletin that day summarized: "In the fighting at the San and Vistula since the end of July, 24.Pzr-Div. led by *Generalleutnant* Reichsfreiherr von Edelsheim, already proven on many occasions, was again outstanding in attacks and repulsing the enemy."

In commentaries on the military history of World War II, H. Wagenheimer indicates that the newly formed Army Corps 17 with 24.Pzr. Div. successfully delayed the Soviet advance between the Vistula and the Carpathians, and E. Bauer wrote of those few days "that after the fall of Rzeszow on 3 August 1944" – my last day but one in action – "great things were expected from Marshal Koniev's Russian armoured corps, but nothing happened, and perhaps one may attribute the sudden pause in battle to the intervention of 24.Pzr.Div."

However, after 24.Pzr.Div. had been mentioned in the OKW report previously at a time when all of it became bogged down in mud and was lost,[1] it occurred to me that a mention of that kind in the circumscribed language of Wehrmacht reports could mean: "This unit was totally wiped out."

17.Army released the following Order of the Day on 8 August 1944:

Soldiers of 24.Pzr.Div!

Today 24.Pzr.Div. is separating from 17.Army in the midst of a decisive mission of attack. True to its cavalry tradition at Landshut and Reichshof, 24.Pzr.Div. covered the advance of 17.Army in exemplary mobile leadership and enabled a secure front to be formed between the Carpathians and Vistula. For ten days the division has been at first east of the Visloka, now north of the Vistula, in bitter fighting against an enemy which had crossed the Vistula. Through its dashing attack at Maydan, and the stubborn resistance at the Szcuzsin bridgehead, the division laid the foundations for the attack for which it has withdrawn today upon leaving the Army Corps. For this fighting with outstanding spirit and morale I express my thanks to the division and

---

1. The Wehrmacht Report of 21 February 1944 stated: "In the southern sector the East Prussian 24.Panzer Division led by Generalmajor Reichsfreiherr von Edelsheim distinguished itself particularly."

its commanders and my recognition, and wish you, soldiers of 24.Pzr. Div., luck and success. Signed Schulz, General der Infanterie.

The medical panzer brought me to the main dressing station, in a barn behind a line of poplars and a couple of small woods close to the battlefield on the edge of the village of Rzyska. Despite the frenetic activity which ruled here, the surgeon arrived quickly, examined me and gave me a tetanus injection. Then a Russian "volunteer" prepared some compresses and put them on the burned skin after which the pain subsided somewhat. The pain was only tolerable to some extent when I held my arms up and moved them backwards and forwards.

Exhausted, I sat with many colleagues in front of the barn and awaited events. The Russian volunteer who first helped treat me said while applying the bandages that she was going to leave the dressing station at the first opportunity to go over to the Russians. She had recognized our situation: "No chance for a victorious end to the war."

A group of walking wounded including myself was assembled for an ambulance ride to a field hospital at Tarnov. Doctors were in attendance there immediately to change dressings. They listened in disbelief to my statement that the Russians were already at Debica. Freshly bandaged, I was put to bed where I told a male nurse how to work my camera, which was still slung around my neck, and with his assistance I had my photo taken all bandaged up in the field hospital.

That night I was in the hospital train. It was made up of new, very modern express coaches with double bunks arranged longitudinally. The surgeon and nurse on this train took care of patients at once: I was told to drink as much as I could. Then I heard from the bed below me a voice of protest: "I am an officer and demand a hospital compartment for officers." This was another experience which showed me that there were officers for whom the kindness of a hospital train was of lesser importance than the class markings on the side of the coach. When the train stopped at Cracow, the complaining officer was removed from the elegant hospital coach.

The injuries I sustained on 4 August 1944 marked the turning point of my life as a soldier. Until then I had followed a long zig-zag course: from here on it would be more richly curved but much shorter – only eight months remained until the capitulation. My friend *Unteroffizier* Armin Stolze with 12.Squadron kept a diary in which he noted: "1–3 August 1944, panzer crews superseded: 4 August 1944, panzer 1241-total loss, commander *Wachtmeister* Schmah wounded: 1211-commander *Oberwachtmeister* Assmann fell in action, *Unteroffizier* Armin Böttger severe burns (face and hands), hospital."

Chapter 18

Reserve Hospital: News of the SS Miracle Weapon

The hospital train passed close to Amstetten (Austria) in Upper Silesia and Czechoslovakia before reaching its destination at Mauer-Öhling. This great curving route took it twice across Germany proper. As men on leave from the front received a parcel each time they crossed the old German frontier, I got two parcels from Red Cross nurses. Through the train window at Mauer-Öhling I saw a large number of these nurses on the railway platform and some ambulances in the background. After a wait I was unloaded with other wounded and transported to the reserve field hospital there. It had taken over various buildings of a former mental hospital in very beautiful parkland. Green pastures, many paths lined with bushes and lots of trees provided a very countrified atmosphere during the finest summer weather. I had arrived at a place where peace and quiet reigned, a place which bode well for a swift recovery.

I found time to read once more: books from the hospital library, and newspapers. In a local Austrian newspaper I read a report by the SS war correspondent Joachim Fernau which made me extremely annoyed. On one page the absolutely honest, realistic portrayal of the retreat on all fronts, the story of the incessant defeats one after another, and on the next page the almost cynical conclusion: approaching victory. Here is the article he wrote under the title *The Secret of the Last Phase of the War*.

29 August 1944. At the latest within six months we shall know what few know today, that the last phase of the war which began on 16 June 1944 has a secret, and that the three months June, July and August truly bear a quite different face than we all believed. This time which we are going through now, right now, is the most dramatic that modern world history could ever experience. Later eras will see clearly and distinctly that it all came down to a matter of millimetres and seconds, though it must have been possible to calculate that Germany would be victorious.

It seems fantastic to imagine that it is so certain, for at the present time the world for us looks quite different. Kharkov fell, Stalino, Dnyepropetrovsk, Uman, Smolensk, Pleskau, Vitebsk fell, the Soviets are coming ever nearer. Kiev fell, Lemberg fell, they have got to the gates of Warsaw, Cracow and East Prussia. Divisions are thrown against them and are forced to retreat, endlessly retreat, regiments are wiped out, vast quantities of materials sink in the Russian mud, aircraft and artillery and panzers are lost; something must finally bring all this to an end. But the next day also brings nothing. Slowly but surely the Soviets constantly advance.

In Italy the ulcer of Nettuno burst, the British marched and marched and marched bringing up their crazy numbers of artillery and aircraft and are now in Florence. On 6 June the invasion began with a raging inferno of bombs and shells, the British and Americans gained a foothold in Normandy, our counter-attacks failed. Without a pause British bombers drone over Germany and destroy our cities. That is how June and July looked.

It must be set out in these cold words, for it is the truth and that is the honour of our soldiers. It is a ghastly picture, but it is false. If we did not know it for ourselves and be able to prove it, Churchill himself would be the best man to teach us, and he would not hesitate, for his sees this picture quite differently too. In six months everybody will know it.

Britain and the United States began the war in 1939, a year which was far from favourable for them. Both States were not ready. The United States was not prepared to go to war officially at all. German superiority was unmistakeable. Britain knew that, but not the extent. To tell the truth their reckoning was inspired and based on statesmanlike strategy dating back to the Pitts; namely by the use of strategy, weaponry or bravery to prevent from the outset an early outcome: the war must under all circumstances be drawn out to the phase of general exhaustion for the final struggle. Thus it took on the character which Britain and the United States desired: the see-saw. We must not forget this concept, to which I shall return soon.

The Führer knew all this. He tried to destroy this plan by defeating the countries which Britain had drawn to it for its own purposes, and to achieve a strategic decision in 1940. We were very close to it, but it failed because the Soviet Union committed the act without parallel of aligning itself with capitalism and entering the war. Britain could breathe again.

That was the situation in 1943. The British and Americans practically put their hands in their pockets and let the war run its course. They achieved superiority at sea and in the air, battered Germany slowly but surely and stayed clear of the main fighting on land. They could just have sat back and waited out the war. Yet something very strange occurred! In 1944 there began an enormous offensive against Germany. Nobody doubted that this was extreme overkill. The British no longer came with a hundred bombers but now with a thousand. They came ashore at Nettuno [Alled landings at Anzio in January 1944], fired off two hundred thousand shells at one sector in a day and made 6 June the day for the general invasion. In the east Stalin attacked with all his reserves. The world was impressed. Nobody noticed, however, that all of this was mighty strange and that these sacrifices at the gates were totally unnecessary if everything was as they said it was. But everything was quite different.

One year before, Churchill already knew what even we ourselves did not. The British Home Secretary Morrison put it into words a few days ago in Parliament. In reply to a question what was up in Germany, he said: "I know of terrible things". The gigantic upgrading of the assault in 1944 was not overkill, but the greatest alarm and panic. I remember very well that the French terrorists decorated the walls last year with the following motto: "1918–1943".

1943 was to have been our 1918. Today I know it was no theory of propaganda, it was a programme, it was the greatest possible need. Churchill knew all about it! He knew dates which not even we ourselves knew and still we do not know today. We found on a prisoner a British newspaper several years old which had a sketch of the V-1, inaccurate, but not by much. When I saw that, it was clear to me how it proves:

1. Churchill knew early on about the coming weapons.
2. He was not able to prevent them being built.
3. He could not build his own before we did.
4. He does not know what the defence against them is.
5. He knew therefore that there would be a date when a third phase of the war began and Germany, just as in 1942, would take the leading role in the war again, and in this phase Germany would be on top.

Just as he knew about the "V-1", so must he also know about other "terrible things". And he knows something else, for him much more to be dreaded. He knows the date. Therefore he wrote "1918–1943", therefore the end – our end from exhaustion – had to be 1943 without fail. The year passed.

We ourselves did not suspect what that meant for Churchill and Roosevelt. Now there was one last chance for them: in the final minutes of their phase of the war to gamble on a desperate joint offensive, and we are expecting it now. If any further proof be needed, Churchill provided it himself in an interview a few days ago. He said: "We must end the war by autumn, or else..." and at that the old gentleman, the arsonist, fell silent.

By autumn, by saying that, we know why we have to make the last great effort. It is not about our forces. In this war we have never given up in a critical situation. We shall pay the last asking price which we have to pay. With all means and forces at our disposal. Victory is actually quite near.

A cynical masterpiece of National Socialist propaganda? With this the propagandist Joachim Fernau, who after the war wrote several popular books (e.g. *Von Arminius bis Adenauer*, and *Rosen für Apoll*), took us for a ride.

In the first days at Mauer-Öhling I was in great pain from my burns. On the third day I had a circulatory problem. Even the first change of dressings caused me such distress that the doctors gave me strong pain-killing injections (a mixture of Scopolamine, Eukodal and Ephetonine). Every morning the nursing sister would greet me with the question what I wanted to eat. I would be given an inventory of foodstuffs and could choose whatever I wanted from the kitchen stock, besides which I had a glass of wine daily and fresh coffee. Whatever I could not do with my bandaged hands and arms a female nurse did for me. This outstanding nursing care led to my being discharged from this wonderful hospital by a "KV-machine" after three weeks.

A "KV-machine" was a doctor or medical commission which examined soldiers unfit for active duty to see if there was any way they could play down the wounds to reclassify them "fit for the front". My premature discharge from hospital did have a silver lining, for the next doctor who examined me in the reserve unit was not happy with my progress and said: "You are not fit for the front" and gave me a KV-2, equivalent to "Fit for garrison duty, Homeland" which prevented my being immediately returned to the frontline.

Discharged from hospital I went on convalescent leave to Freiburg. Since I was a wounded soldier home from the front I enjoyed some privileges over civilians, for example I could go to the head of the queue at the cinema ticket office. At the end of this leave I walked through the well-remembered barrack gates of the panzer depot at Sagan after an eighteen-month absence.

I met my old friend Graf Posadowsky at Sagan. He was now an officer, and had thus risen in the Wehrmacht hierarchy. I sensed at once the chasm opening between us. He had shrugged off his past as an ordinary soldier while I as an *Unteroffizier* remained one. During the long period of time when we had been friends and stuck together through thick and thin, he as an *Unteroffizier* and I as a *Gefreiter* or *Obergefreiter*, we had been far below the bottom rung of the Wehrmacht hierarchy. Now we belonged respectively to different castes and thus our estrangement was probably unavoidable. Upon parting we exchanged a few unimportant phrases, then he glanced at his watch and pronounced the sentence which separated us for ever: "I must see my colonel." Now he had neither time for me nor wished to hear my plea to do something to keep me at Sagan.

Chapter 19

Courier in East Prussia

Instead of being stationed at Sagan I was ordered to Zinten in East Prussia close to Königsberg. "Why does a soldier from southern Baden have to land up at the other end of a diagonal right across Germany?" I thought with displeasure on the journey to Zinten via Posen. I did not know then that in East Prussia the goddess of good fortune had spread her wings practically above me, and I felt this first flap of her wings after I reported to Panzer Unit 10 at Zinten and was asked if I would like to be a courier.

Naturally I accepted at once this chance of a soft number out of the firing line, and soon I found myself making daily journeys by train as if a civilian. I would depart Zinten at 1000 hrs either for Königsberg to the Deputy Commanding General, 1.Army Corps or the Wehrmacht commandant's office, or via Königsberg and Wehlau to Insterburg for the commander of Panzer Troop 1. In my bag I carried mostly secret letters and orders. Thus I was a sort of military postman albeit with the privilege of more freedom and time to myself than other soldiers at the Zinten unit.

That showed itself at reveille at 0600 when the order to get up resounded through the barracks. I could ignore it and turn over for another two hours since I did not have to report to the commander until 0900. The other advantage lay in my destinations. There was a busy rail service between Zinten and Königsberg leaving me with the rest of the day to myself. The journey itself was very pleasant. When the train arrived at Zinten or wherever, I would get into the separate courier's compartment. Should the train lack one I would flourish my courier's certificate and a 3rd class rail pass to the female train guard and join her in her cabin. We always had a good time and often we would loosen up.

For food I received field rations or food coupons on alternate days. Using clever tactics with the waitresses in the eating houses I often got a meal without coupons, or with a discount in coupons. I was especially successful with a salesgirl at a Zinten bakery. She was nothing like so pretty as her colleague at Sagan but made up for it by refusing to accept bread coupons for my purchases, returning the book intact and accompanied by additional bread coupons.

Königsberg had air raids, especially in August 1944 when six hundred

RAF bombers reduced the city and port, already badly damaged, to rubble. For the soldier a stay in this city had no great restrictions, and with sufficient food coupons there was plenty of opportunity to eat in a guest house or be served at table instead of dining in the barracks food hall.

As the Russian Army approached Insterburg, my Insterburg destination office was changed to Allenstein, and so now I shuttled back and forth between Zinten and Königsberg, or Zinten and Allenstein. Depending on the type of train, Zinten to Königsberg took fifty minutes, Insterburg three hours and Allenstein two hours twenty minutes.

Chapter 20

Special Leave: Memories of School, the *Jungvolk* and Hitler Jugend

Freiburg im Breisgau, until then largely spared air raids, suffered a fearsome bomber raid on 27 November 1944. I requested special leave, was allowed to travel at once and so saw for myself the terrible result of this air raid.

I was reunited with my mother, still healthy, and my sister in the undamaged house in Mösle-Strasse, this short leave overshadowed by the destruction of the centre of Freiburg. Many famous buildings, entire trams, Sazl-Strasse and Kaiser-Strasse had been demolished and were now rubble with a narrow path running through. Of many houses now only the walls remained, many crumbling, fronted by a giant heap of rubble. There was a stench of burning. Above the ruins towered the cathedral with its wonderful Gothic spire, miraculously untouched. Of the dentist's surgery in the Stadtgarten district where my sister had been employed, only brickwork was left. When the sirens sounded she had run towards Schlossberg and got to an air raid shelter in the vaults below the rocks there.

I made my way over and through the wreckage to my former school, the Berthold Gymnasium [High School]. It had been destroyed and the city theatre opposite reduced to its foundation walls. I recalled the total of fifty-three impressive performances in this theatre which the girls of the school had staged with the encouragement of a National Socialist cultural organization – *Dornröschen, Maria Stuart, Prinz von Homburg* to the operas *Fidelio, Fliegender Holländer* and *Lohengrin* with the heroic tenor Horst Taubmann. He was the idol of all the girls.

I recalled my schooldays and the many years of highs and lows there, and of my first encounter with National Socialism in the second form (fifth grade). The following year, 1933, a Catholic priest was headmaster of this humanistic high school, but was replaced in 1934 by a teacher who wore the Party badge. He came into class one day and told all boys who were not members of the *Jungvolk* to stand. The majority including myself stood up and the new, strict headmaster, unmistakeably wearing the swastika of the Party member in his lapel, made us fall into a line. I remember thinking that whoever looked and behaved like this must be a Nazi. As he stood before us, tall and erect in a military manner like a Prussian officer, we quaked in our boots. By his demeanour it seemed certain we had done wrong. Then he began: "Why are you not in the *Jungvolk*?" We stammered out our lame excuses.

"Like every German child, a pupil at the Berthold Gymnasium must be a member of the *Jungvolk*. Therefore join immediately!" With this order he left the classroom, but not for long, and soon he was back to repeat the performance. In the end there was no choice and everybody was soon in the *Jungvolk*.

I also remembered very well the tutelage and compulsion with which entry into the *Jungvolk* began. This compulsion and later feelings of oppression accompanied me over the years and increased during the war. Straight away, the *Jungvolk* leaders were up to their tricks. My name was changed to Armin from Hermann, my true first name, because they already had a Hermann. Then during the weekly trips into the countryside we received pre-military training. We learned how to read a map and use the terrain to reconnoitre and storm "enemy positions". We could navigate by compass, knew the Morse code and much else. This service with the *Jungvolk* was a pain. I would much rather have spent my time being out with girls or playing tennis (I was very keen on tennis and belonged to the No 1 junior team at the Freiburg Tennis and Hockey Club), or playing Skat with like-minded people. I wanted to be free to make my own choices and tolerated the compulsion without knowing – and nor did the others – that we were members of an organisation set up by Hitler. We neither knew nor suspected what Hitler intended nor where his organisations would lead us. Doubtless many *Jungvolk* boys, especially those of a patriotic bent, loved rambling, which would last for days or weeks through the Black Forest equipped with a military-type backpack containing a blanket, bivouac sheet and cooking pot secured as per regulations.

Upon reaching the destination we then had to form a community. I was too much of an individualist to take pleasure in this hiking-and-camping existence. Moreover membership of the *Jungvolk* (and later the Hitler Jugend) upset and weighed heavily upon me, particularly the enforced submission to the power and orders of classmates and other juveniles of my own age or just a little older. We had this weird new vocabulary of the Nazi State bristling with terms such as "Community of the Volk", "Aims of the National Revolution", "Unity", "Readiness to Sacrifice" and "Spirit of Sacrifice of the Youth with Proud German Blood, serving the Führer", "Reverence", "Loyalty and Obedience", "Get Rid of all Those Who Rock the Boat" and other such slogans of a schooling in the world view.

One day while cycling to school I was overtaken and stopped by my immediate *Jungvolk* superior. What now? At the time I wore the school cap which had a peak and was made of coloured materials. This cap identified the wearer not only as a pupil at the Berthold Gymnasium, but its colour indicated which form or grade one was in. Thus a sixth-grade student wore a green cap, fifth-grader blue, and so on from red to yellow, black and cardinal. The pupils of the top form (Upper Sixth in Britain) even wore a *Stürmer*, the cap characteristic of the student organisations. These caps expressed individuality and did not fit into the uniform landscape of the Nazi organisations. Until 1935 I had taken great pride in my school caps, now I was ordered never to wear one again.

Corresponding to the Führer's slogan "As hard as Krupp steel, tough as leather", steadfastness played a major role in training, for a hard young lad could be made into a hard soldier. This steadfastness training occasionally assumed undignified forms. During one ramble I was thrown to the ground and pinned down while another boy sat on my nose and farted. Enraged and disgusted, I was more than dejected.

I still did not suspect that such things were a pre-stage of Wehrmacht training in which, as in all Third Reich organisations, the human peculiarities of one's superiors, such as their power complexes, played a fundamental role. After the farting experience I refused to participate in the next weekend ramble. The troop leader wrote at once to my father telling him that I should attend the following ramble in order not to miss the community and comradeship around the camp fire, the most wonderful experience a boy could have.

The *Jungvolk* and Hitler Jugend also influenced the school schedule, for the boys of the *Jungvolk* had Saturday ("State Youth Day") free. In harmony with the aims of the youth organisations, light athletics at school (60-metre sprint, long jump and putting the shot) received more emphasis and boxing was obligatory. Hitler himself was of the opinion that no sport fostered the aggressive spirit so much as boxing did and the "young healthy boy" should learn through boxing "how to take it".

The top boy in our class academically, a student of the classics with above-average achievements in all disciplines with the exception of sport – he never once finished the 50-metre sprint – took a terrible beating the first time he tried boxing. Next day he gave notice of withdrawal and left the school. In the course of time the efforts of the tutors to make the cultural world of the Ancient Greeks and Romans known to their pupils were consistently forced back by a changed emphasis in the subject; in this way teachers with the Party badge and the sports masters now concentrated on gymnastics in Ancient Greece, which was then used to justify a new gymnasium.

After making my way through the rubble-strewn Berthold-Strasse I reached the railway station. Another field of bricks and rubble. The beautiful *Zähringer Hof* hotel in which we had held our school-leaving ball was razed to the ground. In the station ruins my mind returned to my time in the *Jungvolk*. After two years with the *Jungvolk*, by becoming a drummer I had managed to break free of the pre-military and enforced routine with its constant exercises on the land. I carried a large drum – "boom, boom, boom-boom-boom" – which set the pace for the *Jungvolk* troop marching behind the band.

With the drum as the first attribute of the foot soldier, the infantryman in me began to take shape unrecognized. Together with the monotonous tempo I also learned the rhythm of the *Yorckscher Marsch* and to do a drum roll. In front of the ruined railway station I recalled the day when I was a drummer with the *Jungvolk* at the station waiting for a train to pull in bearing the coffins of thirty-two British boys. With their teacher they had wanted to see spring on the Schauinsland in the Black Forest, but had been caught out in their light gear in a snow storm and died.

I must add that whilst in the *Jungvolk* I undertook instruction for my confirmation. The evangelical parson began with the Hitler salute and ended with "Heil Hitler!" For my confirmation I received the impression of Dürer's horse rider with a quotation from the Petrus letter: "Be modest and set your hopes ..."

At age fourteen I was transferred automatically into the Hitler Jugend. Out went the big bass drum, back in came the activities in the countryside: yet even in the Hitler Jugend it was possible to escape them. I transferred to the Motor-Hitler Jugend and obtained a driving licence class 4 for motor-cycles up to 250 cc. Motor-cycling was a fascinating experience for the fourteen-year-old Hitler Jugend boy. It was also the first step towards obtaining special permission for obtaining the driving licence class 3 at age sixteen. During driver training I drove a car through most of those streets which now lay in debris and ashes. At the outbreak of war columns of cars carried out training exercises for a possible emergency evacuation of Freiburg. For this purpose, provided a vehicle was available and not requisitioned, it came with a modest petrol allowance. I had to attach a red triangle to the number plate and exhibit a "P" shield as a learner driver.

In the enormous field of debris which had been the old town of Freiburg, the cathedral, the Swabian Gate and the Martins Gate remained standing. At the latter, below the Reich eagle added in 1902, and which held the coats of arms of Baden and Freiburg in its claws, I saw an inscription which I consider one of the biggest let-downs of the century: *sub umbra alarum tuarum protegenos* ("Under the shadow of thy wings protect us"). Neither the eagle of the Kaiserreich nor that of the National Socialist State did so. Much more did the eagle of the times bring us sorrow and destruction, and for many during the war, death.

Chapter 21

In East Prussia Again

Having returned to Zinten after my special leave there was a major problem affecting my activity as courier. It took a lot of effort for me to force my leave stand-in to relinquish the post. He found being a courier much to his liking and was very opposed to returning voluntarily to the anonymity of the barracks. I reported to the competent captain and reminded him that it was "my job": I was well known to the various offices which I had to visit and had experience as a courier. This resulted in his decision in my favour.

In Zinten, as elsewhere, there were naturally KV-machines, but as a courier, absent every day from the barracks, I was never available to appear for medical examination. I shared an office with an NCO who had lost an eye in the fighting and was wearing a black eye-patch until his glass eye was ready. He was engaged on office duties, and because I had a very good relationship with him, it was my good fortune that he continuously rubber-stamped my papers "Unfit for the front" without my ever having seen a doctor again.

Thanks to my comradely office neighbour and his illegal help I continued with my daily work as a courier carrying secret messages here and there. The last time was 21 January 1945 by car to Allenstein because the train service between Zinten and Allenstein had been suspended. A couple of hours later the Russians took Allenstein with seven tanks, all very low on fuel.

Russians forces were now converging on Zinten and Königsberg, and when they spread out towards Elbing, the ring was tightened and my activity as a courier came to an end. Streams of countless German soldiers, all pulling back, filled the Zinten barracks to overflowing. Nobody knew what would happen next, and there existed a general fear that eventually all able men not actually fitted with artifical limbs or waiting for them and who could fire a gun would be sent to the front for slaughter.

On 27 January 1945 I wrote a letter to my mother franked at Danzig on 9 February 1945, saying: "House to house fighting is raging in Elbing and we do not know whether we shall have to defend the Zinten barracks. As it happens, one of the higher command staffs, (the pro-Hitler *Generaloberst* Rendulic) is here with their *Blitzfrauen* (female signals staff) and where these gentlemen sit is mostly well back from the frontline ("A panzer unit cannot be led from ahead" – A. Stahlberg). I was also not aware then that my East Prussian 24.Pzr.Div. was deployed to protect East Prussia forward of Zinten. During the final phase of the fighting for East Prussia, the division had to withdraw to the southern coast of the Haff, on the beaches between Balga and Rosenberg.

From about four thousand survivors of the division, some five hundred were chosen to attempt to make for Schleswig-Holstein while the remainder faced a more than black future.

In this extremely depressing situation, on parade one day the *Spiess* was looking for a corporal and a squad of men to stand guard duty. He asked each man what his wound was. I reported on my burns but since on the whole I looked quite healthy I received the order to take a platoon to the petrol store outside Zinten and guard it for twenty-four hours.

In an uncertain situation, overshadowed hourly by the threat of being ordered to join the infantry at the front and fight a hopeless defensive battle, it gave me little pleasure to set out on this assignment, but orders were orders and I had to go to the petrol store. When I returned to the barracks twenty-four hours later, my colleagues said, "You lucky bastard. While you were playing sentry a KV-machine was here." Apparently many of the soldiers stationed at the barracks were written up "Fit for the front" and sent there forthwith. Because of the guard duty I had not been present and as a "forgotten man" carried on with my duties with the heap of cripples at the barracks.

This choice of myself by the *Spiess* to be platoon commander caused me to wonder. What had he known in advance? Even more important, had I falsely represented my condition to him? As would prove, this guard duty was a key event in my life.

Next day everyone at the barracks, including women in uniform, was transferred out to a barracks at Heiligenbeil crammed to overflowing. The NCOs occupied quarters as a self-contained unit in a loft directly under the roof. As at Zinten, we heard artillery fire all day, and it was well known that the Russians were quite close to Heiligenbeil. The Red Army had meanwhile reached Elbing, and so we were virtually encircled with an escpe route only towards the Frischer Haff on the coast overlooking a spit of land known as the Frische Nehrung.

Chapter 22

Escaping the East Prussian Encirclement

"How do I find a merciful God?"

Martin Luther

The mood amongst the demoralized garrison in the Heiligenbeil barracks could fall no lower. The situation was the bleakest imaginable. As an example of the generally desperate and depressed frame of mind I mention the reaction to a song rendered with feeling by a corporal to his colleagues around him in the loft: "You should send me no more red roses." To this came the brutal response, "Don't worry, nobody will ever send you any more."

The decisive hour fell on 6 February 1945. Everybody had to be examined by a young medical officer. NCOs and men stood in a long queue before a small table at which the doctor had seated himself. In anxious suspense each related his condition. There followed a cursory examination and then the doctor pronounced his verdict. This was either "Fit for the front" or "Not fit for the front". The Spiess had already confided to me quite simply what I had to do: "Convince this doctor that you are unfit for the front."

"So, what's wrong with you?"

In a convincing tone and knowing that this doctor could not conduct a proper examination, I replied, "Burns face and both hands. I have lost two-thirds of my sight and have myocardiac damage." This latter condition could be serious, but could not be detected by the sort of cursory examination being conducted here. The doctor took out his stethoscope, listened to my heart, sat back behind his table and gave me a penetrating, perhaps uncertain, look up and down. I looked him directly in the eye. Then he murmured so that not only I but also the *Spiess*, standing near the table, could hear: "Not fit for the front". He took a proforma prepared on a typewriter and inserted the word *nicht* before *einsatzfähig* on the paper. Then I was dismissed.

A great weight was lifted my heart. By my deportment and a huge amount of luck I had received this moment important piece of paper for the last three months of the war. Upon my return to the barracks loft when asked by my comrades for my result my answer *"nicht einsatzfähig"* unleashed incomprehension, rage and even hate amongst those who had been declared "Fit for the front" despite visibly serious wounds. "How can a soldier with no visible injuries not be fit for the front?" Measured against the many soldiers there, mutilated and crippled, whom the doctor had declared fit for front duty, his medical opinion was not only false but criminal, but such injustices occur in war. What would the fate be of those "fit for the front"? They would join an infantry unit with no armour, no ammunition to speak of and no hope: the best they could expect was death or Russian captivity.

Next day those unfit for the front were released with orders to reach Danzig via the Frischer Haff and Frische Nehrung. I was with them on the morning of 7 February 1945 as we left Leysuhnen for the ice of the frozen Haff. It was a misty, dismal, rainy day and the view across the ice offered no comfort.

The ice had a covering of water. Thousands of refugees' carts were on it. They were a picture of misery. Delivered a low blow by Fate, forced to leave the Homeland and fleeing over the ice, women, children and old men perched on the overloaded vehicles containing their last possessions, utensils, sewing machines and frying pans. The rain whipped their faces unceasingly and all the time we could hear clearly the artillery fire at nearby Elbing.

What the people of East Prussia went through was unparalleled and indescribable. Women gave premature birth on the ice, old people lay dead on it. Despite the cape around my shoulders the water got through my greatcoat and uniform to my skin. Since I was also wading behind a waggon, my shoes, socks and trousers to above the knees were all soaked, as were those of my comrades. When a break appeared in the clouds Russian fighters and fighter-bombers came and dropped small bombs on the fugitives. These would either hit them directly or crack or hole the ice causing carts and wagons to sink through it. My backpack, filled with personal items of basically no real use, had become very heavy and was pressing on my back. After a few kilometres I had thrown it aboard a wagon near where I was walking. Some time later I noticed it had disappeared. It came as a blow: "Your backpack with your last belongings is gone." Then with relief I saw it being towed along through the water on the ice behind the waggon. It had fallen off but a strap had caught on the axle.

As a result of the bad weather the convoy of refugees advanced only slowly. Avoiding bomb holes in the ice and proceeding through standing water, bunching occurred and endless queues formed. Soldiers and thousands of refugees needed almost a day to cross the frozen Haff. Over the next few days the ice became more brittle and the water level rose. On the evening of the first day after the crossing we reached a small village, Strauchbucht, filled to overflowing with refugees.

There were no lodgings to be had. Because it was still raining and I did not wish to spend the night in the open, I had to be satisfied sleeping in a dovecot. I crawled inside cautiously, followed at once by a mother with her two children who were hungry and crying because of the cold and their wet clothes. The mother could do nothing to alleviate their condition. My own clothing, greatcoat and the two blankets for the floor were soaked and cold. Thus a Prussian corporal fleeing and wet through had only a dovecot in which to spend the night. To any normal soldier it should have long been obvious that we were in the final phase, but there were still those prepared to fight to the last, still believing we would be "victorious".

Nect day we picked up where we left off, always with the dreadful misery of the refugees before our eyes. Once I saw a bicycle resting unchained against a house wall. This would have provided me with an easy way out. To overcome the inner *Schweinehund* and keep plodding with my heavy backpack without a bicycle was no easy task, but I couldn't bring myself to commit the theft.

On the fourth day we reached the Vistula. A really well-built wooden bridge spanned it. A captain was blocking access. I showed him my *"nicht einsatzfähig"* chit. "Give me your paybook!" I felt uneasy watching him flick through it. Then he confiscated it. "Go into the barracks over there!" I was ordered. Now I am done for, I thought, and not just because without my paybook and chit I had no identity documents nor paper to prove I was unfit for the front. In any case the captain could refuse to let me cross the river. After a brief while the barracks began to fill with soldiers who were also deprived of their paybooks. This looked bad. After a half hour or so the officer summoned me. Pressing my paybook and chit into my hand he ordered me to leave with twenty men and report to a barracks at Danzig at 1800 hrs the same evening. I was given the twenty paybooks in a batch.

I read out the twenty names and led the men to the great bridge, passing by the captain without whose authority we could not go. On the other side of the Vistula was a lorry just about to drive off. I ran up to the driver and if he was going to Danzig. When he said yes, I asked if he could take us all with him. He agreed, and gave me a few minutes to address the men.

I called out the name of each and gave him his paybook. "You must report to such-and-such a barracks at Danzig at 1800," I said, and then we boarded the lorry. My God, was I pleased we could cover the last part of the journey in a lorry and not on foot. In Danzig the driver stopped in the city centre. "My heartfelt thanks," I said, and with my pack on my back I headed for the nearest café. It was almost like peacetime in this establishment. For a short while my world changed. I ordered coffee from a waitress who, after my four days on the march, looked especially pretty and desirable. I was soon in conversation with other soldiers and learned that this such-and-such barracks to which I was heading at 1800 hrs was an assembly camp for soldiers being sent to the front. I was told of another barracks where the chances for panzer men to get transport to the west were substantially greater.

With grateful thanks I decided to ignore the captain's order and went to the panzer barracks instead. Panzer men were held here to await transport to the west, and then shipped by goods train first to Neuruppin and then on to Gross-Glienecke near Berlin. In the extensive terrain of the depot we waited in fear of a KV-machine, or whatever other way it was being done here, but after a few days of suspense we were sent to Erfurt.

After the war Hans Riebe, who had also been a 12.Squadron column-leader's radioman, said that after a rearguard action with the remains of 24.Pzr.Div. in April 1945, he crossed the Frischer Haff and got to Schleswig-Holstein with the German Navy. The division was to be re-formed there.

Chapter 23

Courage instead of Obedience

After arriving at Erfurt we hoped we had finally escaped the Russians. Our aim was to become prisoners of war of the Americans. Unfortunately US forces did not move up fast enough, and after a few days I received the order, together with another corporal, to take ten soldiers each back to Silesia and join Schörner's fighting force there. At this time the ring around Germany was being closed ever tighter – and I was supposed to be slaughtered in the last few days of fighting alongside Schörner?

Calmly I considered how I could circumvent this order. Perhaps I should head west. On reflection that seemed too dangerous, for soldiers could be shot on the spot without trial if caught fleeing without orders. Therefore initially there was nothing for it but to proceed as ordered. When I got to the station, however, I fell into conversation with a corporal who told me that 24.Pzr.Div. had an assembly centre near Prague. I told my colleague corporal: "Listen, I'm not going to Schörner, I know him only too well from Nikopol. I've heard there is a 24.Pzr.Div. assembly point near Prague, so I'm going to change trains at Chemnitz and go to Prague. Are you up for it?" He declined as did most of the platoon. After a brief discussion only two agreed to accompany me. The others lacked the courage to deviate from orders. Was this soldierly obedience or "shitting their pants"?

After carefully weighing the possibilities I saw in my refusal to obey orders the best chance of surviving the war. At Millowitz near Prague I found the 24.Pzr.Div. assembly centre. I was greeted with the question "Have you still got your Wehrpass?" I had no idea what this was and so replied, "No, it got burnt."

"OK, you can stay and go with us by transporter train to Panzerkorps *Feldherrnhalle* near Znaim."

At the end of April 1945 sitting in a transport I looked for the last time upon the vehicles of The Jumping Rider, the insignia of 24.Pzr.Div. We clanked right across Czechoslovakia with a stop at Brünn, and then arrived at Znaim three days before the capitulation. As the train pulled in I saw some large crates standing on goods wagons. Soldiers sitting beside me stated naïvely, but in tones suggesting they had certain knowledge: "The Führer's secret weapons are in those crates. Now we can still win the war."

I simply could not understand how at this stage of the war anybody could think we still had a chance of winning. Nazi education and propaganda still bore fruit: a couple of stout crates at a railway station were enough for some soldiers to have the incomprehensible lack of reality to believe that Endsieg remained possible.

We reported to Panzerkorps *Feldherrnhalle* and saw at once that the NCOs bore the *Feldherrnhalle* cuff-title and the blue ribbon with silver eagle, the order for time served, but no front decorations. An NCO nearby sneered: "Look at them, they have two bluebirds but otherwise nothing on the breast." Initially we were left in peace except to report for morning and evening roll-call, after which we disappeared into our quarters. Four kilometres away was a village. I found myself a girlfriend there. She had a radio enabling me to tune in to enemy broadcasts and keep myself abreast of the situation. On 8 May 1945 I learned of the capitulation.

Chapter 24

Flight into US Captivity

At first there was disbelief in my unit that Germany had capitulated. On the afternoon of 8 May 1945 we fell in and an officer told us: "Men, Germany actually has capitulated but we of Panzerkorps *Feldherrnhalle* will form an assembly centre to continue fighting the Russians." Back in our squad-room I enquired of my colleagues, "Do you go along with this assembly centre idea? My only interest is getting to the West." Most of them were now of the view that "We are going West with you."

At dusk we had to parade again, and our pistols were taken from us to be replaced by carbines and field rations. I gave my colleagues the command, "Right, let's go." Of the twenty men in the squad-room who had been all in favour of heading West now that Germany had capitulated, and knew we could not be considered deserters, only three took the plunge. Our goal was the Americans. Constant propaganda had warned us that in Russian captivity we should expect beatings, terror, humiliation and years of misery in banishment in Siberia, and in the end death. Today we know that this was no exaggeration. As prisoners of war of the Americans we were to expect humane treatment according to the conventions of war, and in my own case it was what I received. I was lucky, however, for in many French and US camps there was a deliberate regime of terror, starvation and poor hygiene such that very many thousands of German PoWs did not survive.

The majority of the soldiers at Znaim remained apathetic and submissive. In the village shortly before I had espied a car in a garage. Our carbines gave us a libertine feeling as we broke open the garage doors, climbed into our "requisitioned" vehicle and headed westwards. Although one of my group was a harness-master, he was competent on motor vehicles, and now occupied the driver's seat, but when the car broke down after thirty kilometres and would not restart when pushed and declutched we had to continue on foot. After a short while we tossed our carbines into a drain since they were too much of a burden and kept walking westwards.

Contrary to the seventh paragraph of the last Wehrmacht report of 9 May 1945, we did not lay down our weapons with honour and proudly, and neither did we go bravely and optimistically forward to work for the eternal life of our Volk. We slunk out of a situation which we simple soldiers never wanted in any phase of our lives. After we had dumped our weapons we met a troop with a horse-drawn wagon led by a captain. "May we join you?" we asked.

The captain gave us the once-over from which we could see that he did not like the look of these corporals, who had the appearance of deserters. He took us, but unwillingly. A few hours later at a crossroads we encountered an armoured scout car with a cannon aboard which our harness-master recognized somebody and called out to him, "Take us with you!" Thus we four refugees joined the men perched on the scout car.

It was a straightforward run west and at Linz we crossed the Danube, which became shortly afterwards the demarcation line between the US and Soviet forces. Finally we had reached the US sector where as yet nobody had been appointed to take prisoner the huge streams of German soldiers arriving. The Americans told us to set up camp in a field between two half-built houses and stay there. Now we felt sure the war was finally over and we were numbered amongst those who had come through. We were also happy to have eluded the Russians, who were almost at the Danube, although we did not know then what awaited us at the hands of the Americans. When one thinks how quickly during the war German soldiers (see General Schörner for example), especially in the closing phase, ended up in the machinery of terror set up by the Nazi faithful, or were netted by field-gendarmes and subsequently hanged or shot, then US captivity was ultimately a happy finale.

Daily, hourly, fresh batches of soldiers arrived so that the camp, which was only guarded by one or two GIs, soon had thousands of inmates. At first we got nothing to eat and so went begging for food at the neighbouring houses, but how could they give us anything, they who had almost nothing themselves? The weather at least was pleasant. We built our camp using the construction materials lying around. We drove four posts into the ground, covered them with boarding and roofing felt weighed down with stones. This was our quarters.

Close by were some Waffen-SS who had a big tarpaulin which they spread over their four posts in place of roofing felt. Even in captivity the men of this so-called elite force did not relinquish obedience to orders and drill. Every morning at six they were awoken by a whistle and the call *Aufstehen!* After parading there would be much running to and fro with shouting and banging. They had orders to build a fine chalet from the materials lying around. The drill which had been instilled into them was fully maintained in captivity and none of the SS could, or wanted to, shrug it off.

Despite captivity we all got along, although nobody wanted to join our group, the "layabouts". We spent our time sleeping and resting, for without sustenance it seemed best to conserve one's energies and not move around too much. The banging from our neighbours disturbed us, but soon we were to profit from it. The first order from the US authorities at the camp was to bare the shouler and raise the left arm to reveal the armpit. Tattooed or not? Those with a blood group tattoo were recognized as Waffen-SS and transferred to a special camp for SS men. Their chalet was finished, and as they departed the heavens opened over our camp terrain. We abandoned our primitive quarters and moved into the well-built chalet.

Chapter 25

Released – Home with Anxiety and Luck

On 17 May 1945 the Americans registered us by reference to our paybooks. A US doctor examined the prisoners, who had to line up naked for this purpose. The first thing he did was have another look below everybody's armpit for the blood group tattoo which betrayed the members of the SS. Then he raised the penis of each man with a pencil, gave it a critical stare, took a fingerprint on his examination report, for which he had a stamp pad to hand, and with that we were ready for discharge.

On 21 May 1945 I received my Certificate of Discharge and was loaded with other soldiers aboard a lorry. Most of these lorries had black drivers and went to Stuttgart, Nuremberg or Frankfurt/Main. From there one had to make one's own way. Because I had a trunk with civilian clothing on deposit at Tuttlingen, I gave my destination as Stuttgart. As I climbed on the tailboard of the lorry a GI pointed to my watch. I thought he wanted it as a gift and I responded "No, sir". At this he let fly with a cowboy-style hook to the chin which missed. In bewilderment I dangled the watch before his nose but he had lost interest, and so with my tail between my legs but my watch still on my wrist I boarded.

The journey followed the autobahn but lengthy detours because of blown bridges increased the time taken. On the second day the lorry reached Stuttgart-Degerloch. I told my neighbour, "I want to go to Tuttlingen, where I have a trunk of civilian clothing, so I don't actually need to go right into Stuttgart. I am going to jump off, throw me my bag out." As the lorry reduced speed for a bend I leapt out and the bag followed. A short time later I was on a tram going to Echterdingen. Like all discharged soldiers I had long removed the insignia from my uniform such as the death's head collar patches, shoulder straps, eagle and swastika, medal ribbon, Panzer Badge and Wound Badge. My modest black uniform with trousers tucked in at the ankle resembled a skiing outfit, but despite that even from a distance I was obviously a discharged soldier. In the tram a friendly soul asked me at once, "Have you got your French discharge papers?"

"No," I replied.

"You have to have them, or the Moroccans, really nasty pieces of work, will take you immediately to a French PoW camp."

"Where does one get them?"

"From the French *Kommandantur* in Stuttgart."

My annoyance at having gone the wrong way can be imagined. "*Scheisse,* I jumped off too soon, and I could have gone to the centre of Stuttgart all the way by lorry!" When the tram stopped I took one going the other way. I soon found the French military governor's office, and a very polite German-speaking French officer stamped the back of my US discharge paper and hand-wrote upon it *Autorisé à rentrer à son domicile*. "It is asking a lot to find a Moroccan who speaks English", he explained. I nodded, and he went on, "You're out of luck, a US lorry with discharged German soldiers was just here, and those who wanted to go to Freiburg could transfer to a French lorry for the journey." Annoyed and disappointed at losing the chance of a direct run to Freiburg because of my premature initiative, I left the French government building. I took a tram back towards Echterdingen and afterwards Shanks's pony.

The Swabian farmers whom I met on my wanderings were unbelievably hospitable. At nearly every house I was asked "Are you a discharged German soldier?" and when I admitted the fact they would generally invite me in and after hearty greetings offer me a full platter of food with plenty extra to stuff in my bag for later. I spent a night at one farmer's and in the morning saw in the distance the Hohenzollern fortress. By midday it was on my left and in the evening far behind me in the distance.

I was very reluctant to step up the pace: despite my French stamp I could not be sure the Moroccans would let me pass. I did not wish to take any more risks. Moroccans blocked the streets into every locality, and so I gave every village a wide berth. Once in woodland I saw two Frenchmen. My heart hammered as I threw myself into the bushes in fear. Fortunately they neither saw nor heard me. And it continued like that all the way to Tübingen where a French officer checked my papers on the street and let me pass.

On the third day I reached Tuttlingen, found my trunk where I had deposited it and changed into civilian clothing. To finish my journey a French sergeant on a service run to Freiburg gave me a lift in his car. In Freiburg I discovered that discharged soldiers who had got into the French lorry at Stuttgart, which I had missed by my premature action, were taken straight to a French PoW camp for a further six-month stay. Thus on the very last stage of all, my goddess of fortune protected me. I had survived the war and got home safely! After reporting to the French *Kommandantur* and to a German service office in Freiburg, my life as a soldier came to an end.

May 8th 1945 was the day of total defeat and the misery of the defeated. Countless refugees had lost their Homeland, and many of my 24.Pzr.Div.

could not return to East Prussia. From that date however we were free of the pressures of war and the many-sided compulsions of the Wehrmacht. Now one could finally take his fate in his own hands and decide for himself what he wanted to do. In retrospect the primary and overriding desire for oneself, as also for the generations to come, was to never again have to go through such an appalling time.

Whilst during action at the front in a brutal war "come through it and survive" played the decisive role, the following illustrations provide a view of the pauses between the fighting and the many experiences away from it. Especially notable was the difference in uniform worn by the soldier at the front, at home and during the transporter journeys. The miscellany of uniforms worn by troops at the front bore no resemblance whatever to the attractive panzer uniforms so admired in the cinema newsreels. During the fighting, every panzer man might get into a tank wearing no military apparel at all, but on reporting for home leave he had to be dressed in a uniform conforming to regulations.

As a young panzer soldier I accompanied a wide variety of panzer transports to Italian destinations. I was in France, reached Vienna, Bucharest, Kirovograd, Nikopol, Odessa, Jassy and returned to Berlin via Königsberg, from there reaching my home town Freiburg im Bresigau via Brünn. The many travel and transport experiences in many countries and with their inhabitants was extraordinarily impressive and would have been impossible at that time if one had not been in uniform.

The yearning for women played a special role too: the approach, chat, getting to know them and finally the desire for more! There would be contacts on a railway journey with a female train guard or a Red Cross nurse during her turn of duty at a railway station, in a soldiers' hostel and also in a field hospital. In one of many towns with some gall one might make an acquaintance on the street or in a bar. When I went up to a young woman camera in hand and made clear that I wanted to photograph her because she was so pretty, then there would rarely be a problem.

Almost every soldier smoked. Cigarettes were issued with the rations. Amongst the daily smokers were those who preferred a pipe or cigar. The photographs on the pages following are memories "to keep track of the traces".

Chapter 26

The Transition from Wartime Existence

T he end of the war brought a clearly perceptible point of transition to the lives of people in Germany. Most of all for discharged professional soldiers it was especially difficult. Long-serving senior officers returned to the classroom, and the *Spiess* who once had so much power lost his farm in East Prussia and now had to earn his money on the land as a farm labourer. Not everybody could make the transition to simple, everyday existence who once had had the privileges which rank insignia and decorations on the uniform brought with them, but all received, as Richard von Weizsäcker put it, the priceless opportunity of freedom. The military way of expressing things became a thing of the past.

And myself? Going back to school, which I had hoped for during the war, was no longer open to me. I had left school in 1940 with the ambition of becoming a dental surgeon. While serving with Panzer reserve unit 15 at Sagan, on 26 February 1943 I submitted a request for leave to study dentistry at the University of Freiburg. I suffered from a stomach complaint which had resulted in my being written up as only "Fit for garrison duty, Homeland", therefore not fit for the front.

Stupidly I had chosen the wrong discipline. I could have obtained leave to study medicine, but not dentistry. This I did not discover until later. And now, in 1945, it was no longer taught at Freiburg, which lay in ruins, including the section of the university with the dental clinic. This was the situation when I saw my mother and sister again on 25 May 1945. Arriving home, I went as usual to the kitchen door at the rear of the house in order to embrace my mother. I went into the kitchen and was surprised to find it full of strangers. "Your mother lives upstairs," I was told. She had moved into the upper portion of the house with my sister after the big air raid when there was a severe housing shortage and she took in two bombed-out families. At this first joyful reunion with my mother and sister, at last the moment had come for which I had yearned so long in uniform: to be at home in peacetime.

Initially it was not easy to find the right path out of the chaos. We soldiers certainly trembled with the fear of death during the fighting but, as would be shown, we did not fear to live, as the National Socialists would have us believe in 1943. The main thing now was a trade. First one would have to get used to the new "rulers". The French occupation force was hostile. They often tormented the local populace and pursued a harsh denazification policy. Houses and flats were requisitioned. They would seize vehicles and motor-cycles, or French soldiers would simply steal them on the street. Our car had long been French booty. A few days later after my return, when a French officer came to the door and demanded our garage, we were relieved that he hadn't come for the whole house. We had to clear out all the garden tools at once and also the wood supply which my sister and I had cut down in the Sternwald with great effort and no proper food, and had then sawn to size and stored in the garage.

There was far too little to eat. Therefore in those first months after the war we used to tour for food. Rationing was so tight that we had no option but to visit the hoarders in the countryside, or better put "descend upon them". Often we were reduced to begging at farmhouse doors. If we got a litre of milk that was a good result. If one had something to barter, then the chances were naturally better of his bringing home some butter or a staple food such as potatoes or bread. These tours were almost impossible to make without a bicycle. My old school bike was fairly serviceable but spent much time upside down for repairs to the inner tubes.

In those early postwar weeks there was no question of studying anything, and I looked for some kind of activity connected with dentistry on the technical side. There was a dentist who had been a freemason in the same lodge as my father. In the Herdern he had a house where he re-opened his practice after losing everything in the big air raid. His cousin, also bombed-out, who had been President of the Chamber of Dentists of South Baden, also practised in the house at Herdern. A few more houses down was the villa requisitioned by General Pène, the French administrator of South Baden. A dental technician worked in a small laboratory annexed to the practice, and I was able to start there at once as his assistant.

The practices of the two cousins were cut differently. My boss, who spoke perfect French, handled the French occupation authorities from General Pène downwards. As well as people of standing in Freiburg, large numbers of farmers and their wives came to the surgery. Now the barter situation was reversed. While I had to go to these people and beg, they came to my boss with a sack on the pannier of their bicycles, mainly offerings of poultry, which quickly found their way into the dentist's kitchen. Once I had proved my worth to the practice I was invited to dine at midday and so profited from this barter. The academic elite of the university attended the cousin's practice.

To re-establish the study of odontology it was necessary to rebuild. The big air raid had almost completely destroyed the Pre-Clinical Institute. The important rooms at the Anatomical Institute had no plaster, windows or heating. During the winter semester the students and tutors sat in the summer rooms in heavy clothing, particularly Wehrmacht greatcoats without the insignia. The former inn "Zum kühlen Krug" in the Günterstal was rented and converted into a dental clinic with new equipment.

Admission to odontology was difficult, not only because the number of beginners was limited to ten, but applicants with the "War *Abitur*" had to complete two terms of introductory teaching to catch up. A commission determined which applicants could be admitted to medicine or dentistry without it. These were mainly people with a very good overall *Abitur* pass mark. I was not amongst this preferential circle and in the opinion of a member of the commission, Professor of Physiology Hoffmann, had to do the two terms. Two other commission members, the historian Professor G Ritter and the Senior Director Studies, Breithaupt, were patients of my boss, and he brought "pressure to bear" on my behalf.

Thus a letter arrived from Professor Ritter as chairman of the commission approving my admission to odontology without sitting the two terms. Another circumstance from my work as a dental technician proved very favourable. Dr Hauser was President of the Chamber of Dentists and very close to university lecturer Dr Rehm who until the end of the war had been senior surgeon at the Berlin Dental Clinic. Rehm had been called to a full University professorship and lodged with Dr Hauser, who introduced me to him as his dental technician. With other professors we then set about scouring the ruins of the former dental clinic in Albert-Strasse for serviceable instruments and equipment. During the first semester the students were obliged to spend fifty-six hours in the various buildings removing rubble, cleaning bricks and so on. I continued to work as a dental technician with Dr Hauser and studied in the evenings and at night for a while before devoting myself fully to the study of odontology.

The lectures and courses in dentistry began in the 1946 winter semester. Professor Rehm noticed my technical work and offered a colleague and myself the opportunity to work for the clinic as technicians in the holidays and be excused the second technical course. I agreed at once, and at the end of the holidays he proposed that I work as an auxiliary instructor during the second course.

In the first couple of weeks of study the student or his parents had to pay for lectures based on the hours attended, although this would be waived if the family was in difficulties, or if the student sat two examinations in the same term. A commission decided what the student should pay. As my mother was only in receipt of a small pension and my earnings as a technician were modest, it was a great relief to have the chance to sit the two examinations, though it required intensive concentration on the subjects involved. After the examinations I was made a voluntary unpaid assistant at the Freiburg Dental Clinic under Professor Rehm.

My life was changed completely when Professor Häupl entered my working life. He had worked in Norway, then as head of the Dental Clinic in Prague before being called to Berlin in 1943. After the war he relinquished his chair in Berlin for Innsbruck where he took over the University Clinic. Here he wrote a well-known two-volume manual of dentistry. On the basis of his extensive experience he was the only odontologist in a position to publish such a comprehensive work. In 1951 he accepted a call to Düsseldorf where the Medical Academy needed a man of his standing for the Chair in Dentistry. When the Culture Ministry made him Professor and Director of the West German Kieferklinik, he needed an assistant to whom he could entrust direction of the dentures division. He asked Rehm for his advice, and I was recommended. On 1 November 1952 I took over the department in Düsseldorf. In the period leading up to my appointment I had been the guest assistant in Basle with Professor Sprenger, a very important Swiss dentures manufacturer and scientist.

My time in Düsseldorf with Häupl was marked by a very close tutor-pupil relationship. He became my role model and father-figure. I went to many conventions with him, first to listen and later to deliver addresses of my own. These conventions were milestones in my early scientific career. It was through the great influence of Häupl and Rehm that I set out on the road to being a university lecturer. In the years between 1952 and 1968, Düsseldorf was transformed from a field of rubble into a fascinating city, and although I dreamt for years of being recalled to Freiburg, I turned down the opportunity when it finally arose and remained as Professor in Düsseldorf.

In the final year of my Düsseldorf clinical career I had the pleasure of my daughter attending my lectures, as had my wife before her, and she passed the course. This was within the framework of my main mission to train the next generation and take responsibility for it – the crowning act of my career.

In 1978 I was honoured to receive for German-Italian collaboration the Service Order of the Italian Republic with the title *Commendatore*, awarded me by Italian President Pertini. Thus the former Wehrmacht corporal became an honorary staff officer!

Chapter 27

The Question of the Simple Soldier's War Guilt

After the war I cast my experiences as a soldier completely from my mind. I had other matters to attend to: to learn my profession and prove myself competent in it. I simply had no time to remember the Wehrmacht. I had arranged my wartime photos in albums in chronological order, but I seldom looked at them. It was not for many years that I really thought about the war. It came suddenly to a head during a television discussion about trivial literature of the Second World War when an intolerably arrogant critic (a private publisher of his own work) stated that even the simple German soldier was not free of "war guilt". Other hosts of political TV magazine shows now discuss this question as if they possess the final valid codex of behaviour for young soldiers in the Hitler Reich.

What these people find impossible to grasp is the fact that in any army of the time there was a compulsion to follow orders before which one had no option but to bend. In this connection the former President of Bavaria, Stoiber, explained: "It is dishonest to judge yesterday's events with today's knowledge." More and more we see nowadays historians with a Left-oriented agenda burrowing away into the Wehrmacht, particularly those from the Military History Research Department.

Wolfram Wette, who with a number of colleagues instituted a discussion in the *Die Zeit* newspaper about the blood which 6.Army at Stalingrad trailed behind it, attacked the former Federal Chancellor Schmidt, a man with some Jewish blood, for not admitting that he knew anything at the time about the crimes of the Wehrmacht and the systematic murder of the Jews. A short time later Wette had published in the *Frankfurter Allgemeine Zeitung* (FAZ) an article entitled *Die Legende von der sauberen deutschen Wehrmacht* ("The Myth of the Clean German Wehrmacht"). In this he condemned the generals and their "command assistants"(!) for their incomparably greater culpability in the war of annihilation than the simple soldier.

In response I asked him in a letter how all the simple soldiers, who had no say in anything, could have guilt transferred to them. "What do you think would have happened if I had told my panzer commandant, 'Stop here, I want to get off.' Or on the morning before an attack I had informed my squadron sergeant-major 'I shan't be taking part in this attack today because I do not want any of the guilt for it to rub off on me.' We knew only too well how a General Schörner would have dealt with such nonsense.

General von Manteuffel, holder of the Knight's Cross with Oak Leaves, Swords and Diamonds intervened once in court-martial proceedings. One night a Soviet scouting party had captured a German corporal and another soldier. Two sentries had failed to shoot and did nothing to raise the alarm to free the captured men. Manteuffel ordered the two sentries to be arrested and court-martialled. The defence was that the senior sentry of the two had fallen asleep at his post, and for this he received two years' imprisonment.

At this point Manteuffel intervened and ordered the death sentence to be substituted, as a result of which the sentry was shot by firing squad on 13 January 1944. After the war Manteuffel was found guilty of bringing about a miscarriage of justice (G. Fraschka, see Bibliography) but because he had acted from pure motives he was only sentenced to two months' imprisonment. He justified himself by explaining that soldiers at the front had the right to, and expectation of, protection from their military leaders, and the sentry who dozed off merited the harshest punishment. This thinking was correct from the purely military point of view but might not please the humanitarians of today.

A former naval judge, H. Filbinger, who sentenced a man to death at the end of the war, also justified himself without regrets: "What was right then cannot be wrong today:" Filbinger, Manteuffel and the rest saw their honour in absolute obedience to orders and severe punishment for offenders, and not primarily in their own responsibility to their subordinates.

Later the founders and patrons of the Institute for Social Research, Hamburg, Jan Philipp Reemtsma with H. Heer and others, took over the role of Chief Inquisitor with their exhibition "War of Annihilation – Crimes of the Wehrmacht, 1941–1945". The purpose of the exhibition was to show through the use of documents, some of dubious provenance, that the Wehrmacht had undertaken a war of annihilation and committed atrocities. Today nobody can doubt that even the Wehrmacht was entangled in criminal orders and was guilty of war crimes.

An accompanying letter to the exhibition states that it is not the intention to precipitate a belated and all-inclusive judgement on a whole generation of former soldiers. It may not be the intention, but it is the case. They start out by criticizing the photography of the postwar years where the symbols of National Socialism do not appear together with those of the Wehrmacht. Swastika and Iron Cross, harmoniously united in the Iron Cross First Class, were "carefully separated so as to fabricate acceptable memories" they say, and then they go on to allege that Wehrmacht soldiers took part in these crimes as perpetrators or accomplices, onlookers or amateur photographers. Moreover they point out that in field-post letters, soldiers describe the yellow of the sunflower fields, goose fat and poultry requisitioned from the farmer, but not the bloody massacres and mass shootings.

Thus it was reported of Sixth Army for example: "One remembers it as the army left in the lurch by Hitler, but what did Sixth Army do on its way to Stalingrad? It was one of the leading obedient executors of the National Socialist policy of conquest, and even had amongst its number Henning von Tresckow, one of the 20 July conspirators but responsible for engaging the partisans. A glance at various stages of the advance shows that the fighting troops were just as involved in the crimes of the war of annihilation as the units of the Army areas to the rear."

Now at the time I was not with 24.Pzr.Div. attached to Sixth Army. Comrades who were there have reported the direct opposite: they sat in their panzers, saw only neighbouring panzers and then enemy soldiers and tanks or guns ahead, and above them the wide heavens of Russia over the endless steppe. They fought in conditions of deprivation, and as the following makes clear were always ravenously hungry. When General von Lenski, divisional commander of 24.Pzr.Div. asked a haggard, bearded soldier "What would you like for Christmas?" the man, who had his own farm in East Prussia, replied, "A slice of bread, Herr General." This quote shows that the soldiers there had quite different things on their minds.

The exhibition forgot to mention that the "criminal" soldiers of the fighting units were supplied daily with large quantities of cigarettes mostly of the Reemtsma brand. Many young soldiers became smokers for this reason, while the number of chain-smokers increased dramatically. The "Wehrmacht Exhibition" discredits soldiers and separates them spiritually from their honour. In a reader's letter to the FAZ (*Frankfurter Allgemeine Zeitung*) of 14 July 1999, K. D. Bock drew attention to another aspect: "It is a macabre fact that with the money earned by a businessman and supporter of the system in the Third Reich from manufacturing Reemtsma cigarettes, his heir patronizes the military consumers and cuts them off from their honour. Probably in no other country on Earth would it be thinkable, that a country's own soldiers should be so defamed systematically by an exhibition of this kind."

Meanwhile two foreign historians (Musial and Ungvary) have pointed out to the exhibition managers such a huge number of errors, mistakes and improper assertions as to be a crushing condemnation of it. The only similar kind of things to date have been the State-linked disinformation campaigns (FAZ 22 October 1999). In the same newspaper on 5 November 1999, in his article "The Myths of Reemtsma", Ungvary made his position clear: "Therefore it is impossible to construe the Wehrmacht as the total embodiment of Hitler's ideology without making things up."

The former Federal President Richard von Weizsäcker, himself an officer who in the closing period of the war fought with the remnants of 24.Pzr. Div., stated of this exhibition: "I do not share the opinion of the exhibition organizers regarding the crimes of the Wehrmacht. Undoubtedly there were war crimes within the Wehrmacht sphere of responsibility. It is right that we do not close our eyes to it no matter how hard it is to do so. On the other hand there is a danger in connection with the exhibition that an all-inclusive judgement will be made which cannot find support historically, morally or in human terms."

The former Interior Minister Schily (SPD) decline to designate the Germans as the "perpetrator Volk". The Second World War began with Germany but the label "perpetrator Volk" would be wide of the mark, he said (Deutschlandfunk).

A totally biased book by the Israeli historian Omer Bartov which appeared at the same time talks of the "barbarizing" of German soldiers on the Eastern Front. He takes as an example 18.Pzr.Div. which according to him throughout 1942 in their "desert zone" undertook the summary shooting of suspects. Although the unit had received express orders to hand over all suspects to the police, apparently the murders continued unchecked. Then he comes up with the assertion that there was almost no doubt within the military and political hierarchy of the Third Reich that both the ranking officers and the men were totally loyal to Hitler. As a member of 24.Pzr.Div. I have to say that I must have been in another war. I was also neither a Nazi *Obergefreiter* nor a Nazi *Unteroffizier*.

Outside Germany the assessment of the German soldier is generally different. Ph.Masson's work *Die deutsche Armee* not only describes the course of the war, victories and defeats, strategy and tactics, strengths and weaknesses of the military leadership, battle conditions and the standard of morale, but he admires the achievements of the German soldier, his exceptional readiness to fight and make sacrifices, while deploring the tragic involvement of the generals in the "War of Hitler's World View".

In the Düsseldorf *Rheinische Post* of 6 May 1998 there appeared an interview with the world famous violinst Yehudi Menuhin on the subject of the Third Reich. To the reporter's question "Can we fix the blame?" he replied, "Of course. We are all equally guilty. Fifty years ago it was thought that the Germans were the devil. And in fact they were, but they were not the only ones. After the war it was discovered that Stalin was just as brutal as Hitler. And there were also brutal Jews. One should reflect on that, otherwise it is the end of the world."

Especially detestable was the cynical conduct of the Nobel Prize winner for Literature Günter Grass, exposed by the well-known journalist Hellmuth Karasek in an article in the newspaper *Welt am Sonntag* of 13 August 2006 under the title "Moral Apostle with Gaps of Memory". When US President Ronald Reagan and the Federal Chancellor went to military cemeteries where Waffen-SS men are also buried, Günter Grass criticized this in a violent outburst of indignation. He forgot to mention that he himself had been a member of the Waffen-SS, a fact not unearthed until the archives of SS membership were declassified.

The former French President Mitterand spoke of the courage of the German soldier in the Second World War (at which there was a violent backlash in Germany – where else could it have come from?). On the death of the former U-boat commander Otto Kretschmer the British *Daily Telegraph* ran an eight-part article about his life. S. Brandsahr, a former major in the British Army, expressed concerns about the Wehrmacht Exhibition. He respected the soldiers of the Afrika Korps for their bravery, professionalism and the honourable way in which they conducted themselves.

As against this there comes the objection from the German opposition that it was very different in Russia, to which one may respond that the enemy there was very different, a brutal enemy, and this brings into the argument the influence of the world about us on the behaviour of people and the psychology of the soldier.

The weakness of the case made by the "German opposition" lies on the one hand in its ignorance of what soldiering is, and on the other in concentrating solely on one aspect of war, the atrocities. Thus they only seek the negative, the hallmark of their training in History. What they omit from their portrayal and evaluation is the enormous influence of an environment changed by war, life in uniform, in a group, the soldier's obligation to duty and to obey, his anxieties and the polyphony of suffering.

How did the soldier think during impressive and oppressive experiences, what latitude did he have in obeying orders, how did he think in action when under accurate enemy fire or during a night raid just when he thought he finally had a quiet moment to eat? Did he ever consider refusing an order? Nobody asks these questions about his thinking, conscience and to a certain extent his psychology as a soldier.

War is always cruel and brings suffering and death to countless people. Even in so-called righteous war to drive out an invader, from Arminius against the Romans to the wars against Napoleon, innocent German children were misused as soldiers and drawn into "guilt" and to their doom. As I did, they yearned for a life in freedom.

The world of model-making has a quite different approach to warfare.

So many years after the war, interest in the machines of war and military vehicles such as panzers of all kinds and figures of officers and political leaders remains. There is a wide choice on offer, particularly from foreign firms, and many pictorial and textual magazines about the Second World War. In the Japanese series *Sturm und Drang* I came across a coloured sketch of my panzer 1241 from the year 1943. The text was in Japanese but I recognized my vehicle number 85096, proving that the author had relied on my book for his pattern.

The Japanese firm Tamiya even included my panzer 1241 in its model building programme. Now anybody can build on the 1:35 scale a model of my panzer which saw action in Russia. Noticing the panzer-dog Tapsi of 1241, the firm designed a model SP-gun as used by 9. and 11.Squadrons/24. Pzr.Regt. and provided it with a small dog.

In this connection a model builder wrote: "I decided on a vehicle of 24.Pzr.Div. based on finding a picture of it in a book by Armin Böttger. In his book there is a really big picture of a Kübel of 24.Pzr.Div. It is the car of the 1a clerk. Despite having a tow-rope over the number plate, the mark WH-1477510 can be seen." That is the number used by Tamiya in its model kit.

Martin Walser says at the beginning of his novel *Ein springender Brunnen* that when something is past, a man is no longer the man to whom it happened. This is pertinent to soldiers of the last war, marked by the environmental experiences of a murderous event under a criminal dictatorship.

Soldiers of a division who experienced the war together built a community with a feeling of belonging which endures to the present day. Thus it is only logical that members of 24.Pzr.Div. and Pzr.Regt.24 should attend reunions. Such reunions are still sharply criticised today by the German opposition. At the meetings of my Pzr.Regt.24 a small crowd turns up which has dwindled yearly. Everybody in this community went his own way after 1945 and proved that he was able to use the freedom offered to him.

For the participants at these reunions the important highpoint is the wreathlaying ceremony at a war memorial to remember fallen comrades. These comrades alongside whom we had to fight in war, who were with us and around us and to whom it was not granted to survive, gave their young lives for their belief in a Fatherland which today tolerates the revilement of its soldiers.

At these reunions one meets old comrades with whom one went through thick and thin in 24.Pzr.Div., and who were also lucky enough to come through: and also former officers, who can report about events at a higher level. Thus *Rittmeister* Böke (in action on the Western Front) related a telephone conversation with his commander-in-chief, *Feldmarschall* Model, about the "Panther" of his unit which could not go through a narrow cutting because the panzer was too wide. Arrogant, obsessed with his own power, Model shouted through the mouthpiece at the oficer, "If you do not get it through the cutting I shall sentence you to death!" Böke, irritated because Model had ordered the impossible, thought to himself, "If he gives another order punishable with death for non-compliance I shall desert."

The former commander-in-chief of the Division, Reichsfreiherr von Edelsheim, spoke about the last days of the war. The commander of Twelfth Army, General Wenck, had sent him to the Ninth US Army to negotiate the capitulation. For this purpose he crossed the Elbe twice in an amphibious vehicle. The US commander was prepared to allow all soldiers who could manage it to cross the Elbe westwards, and even take their wounded with them, but he refused absolutely to let refugees cross. Von Edelsheim said that this mission was the worst in his life as a soldier.

Von Christen, former General Staff Officer 1a of the division, had a rich fund of stories to relate. He was the senior of three officers at the OKH Operations Division involved in an incident which highlighted the misuse of power by Hitler, the central destructive factor in his military planning.

At the beginning of 1945 the entire Eastern Front had begun to collapse. *Oberstleutnant* von Christen, who was serving at the OKH HQ at Zossen south of Berlin, received the report that Warsaw was about to fall. He passed this information to Oberstleutnant von dem Knesebeck, 1a at Operations Division, who in turn notified *Oberst* von Bonin, head of communications.

The three officers accepted that Warsaw could not be held and reported the situation to Guderian, Chief of the General Staff, who agreed to their proposal that the remaining German forces in Warsaw should be withdrawn. When Hitler discovered that Warsaw had been evacuated without his consent he flew into a rage and accused the three officers at Zossen of treason. They were arrested in the following way. Higher Staffs worked into the early hours. On this occasion Bonin stated that the previous day had been his birthday, but he had forgotten it because of the pressure of business. Now he ordered up the champagne for a toast.

At that moment General Meisel entered the map room to effect arrests accompanied by three Staff officers wearing steel helmets and carrying machine-pistols. Meisel asked *Oberst* von Bonin for his name. He replied, "You already know it and now we are having our champagne." Von Christen, von dem Knesebeck and von Bonin were arrested, leaving the Operations Division without its senior officers as the Russians first set foot on German soil. This accelerated the chaos of defeat. Von Bonin was handed over to the SD and spent the rest of the war in a concentration camp. Knesebeck fell at the front. Von Christen was rigorously interrogated by Kaltenbrunner, head of the SS-RSHA and then released.

Dr Hubertus Schulz, an officer with 24.Pzr.Div. reconnaissance, was wounded at Stalingrad and afterwards reassigned as Chief Inspector, Panzer Reconnaissance Training Division at Insterburg. Major von Hösslin, commander of this division, recruited him to the military resistance and in February 1944 at the General Army Office in Berlin, Schulz had a conversation with the Chief of Staff, *Oberst* Graf von Stauffenberg. The task of the Insterburg division in the event of a coup was to occupy the Gau and Government offices, other public buildings and the telegraph office at Königsberg. In July 1944 Schulz was sent to the front. Hösslin was arrested a few days after 20 July and sentenced to death. He was hanged on 13 October 1944. Hösslin kept silent throughout his interrogation and so Schulz escaped notice.

During one of our reunions, retired Bundeswehr Generalmajor Gerd Schultze-Rhonhof delivered an address. Along with the content of his speech, it was a great experience for his listeners to know a general who had proved his courage and been forced to accept early retirement. These were the circumstances: About two years before the general's dismissal, a social pedagogue and conscientious objector had distributed stickers with the Tucholsky quote from 1931, "Soldiers are murderers." It was meant as a pacifist statement, but he was charged with defamation of the Bundeswehr and convicted in a lower court. The conviction was quashed on appeal by the Federal Constitutional Court, which ruled that all soldiers may be called murderers. This was not the first time that the highest organ of the German judiciary had exposed itself to ridicule.

In the subsequent lively criticism of this verdict, members of the Bundestag spoke out. The ruling "damaged society" (Kinzel); was "a scandal" (Genschel); "a slap in the face" (Opel); "a disgrace to German justice" (August Thinowitz), "seriously damaging" (Scholz) and "unacceptable" (Defence Minister Rühe). Even the Federal Chancellor found the ruling "deeply wounding".

Minister Blüm, whose brash outbursts as Minister of Health still resound in my ears, saw it a different way. Because soldiers of the Wehrmacht held out for so long, this enabled the concentration camps to remain open correspondingly longer, thus establishing a direct link between the Wehrmacht and the death camps.

It is true of course that the Wannsee Conference protocols state: "The beginning of the major evacuations will be largely dependent on the military situation", but one cannot read into that an order to the Wehrmacht to hold the front as long as possible and enable the chimneys of Auschwitz to keep smoking.

Not all roads lead to Auschwitz! (J. C. Fest). In order to clarify his meaning, Blüm postulated that: "Whether someone served Hitler in a concentration camp or at the front is only a minor matter of degree in my eyes." Rolf Hochhut countered this: "No, there can be no qualitative comparison. The murderer in the death camps was there to avoid fighting at the front, and to prove himself in Hitler's eyes, where he only had to murder unarmed people."

In the framework of the lively criticism of the "Soldiers are murderers" ruling, Generalmajor Schultze-Rhonhof condemned it as "absurd" and so "deeply dishonourable" as to have its equal in comparing the Federal Constitutional Court to Freisler's People's Court. The Defence Minister, Rühe, was not amused, but instead of doing his real duty towards the military as Minister of Defence, he satisfied himself by sending Schultze-Rhonhof into retirement.[1]

During the 1990s I visited those areas and locations where I was stationed as a soldier or was on active service (with the exception of Russia and Rumania). Everywhere I went I knew exactly where I was because so little had changed. The town hall at Brionne was no more, but I quickly found the seed shop, the parade ground at Epaignes, the souvenir shop at Lisieux, the Deauville casino and the highway from Parma to Bologna. The seafront at Viareggio is now overwhelmed by mass tourism with its endless deck chairs and beach umbrellas. I even came across electric locomotive E44084 which had pulled our transport low-loaders from Augsburg to Innsbruck.

The spot where I crossed the Vistula on 10 February 1945 was no problem to identify. Although the wooden bridge has gone its concrete supports remain. I looked at the free ferry for vehicles over the river and wondered why the Poles had not simply built a new bridge there after the war.

The barracks at Sagan are unchanged – soldiers look out of the windows, adorned with flowers, and the girls wait outside the barrack gates as they did in 1941–43. On the roundabout before the barracks is a Russian T-34. The city centre of Sagan is much changed but the station looks precisely as it does in my 1943 photograph. I was able to show my wife the sector of terrain between Milec and Debica where my panzer was destroyed on 4 August 1944: the row of poplars was still there and even the barn where

---

1. In retirement, Schultze-Rhonhof has written several books, the best known of which is his *Der Krieg der viele Väter hatte*, English title with the same publisher *The War That Had Many Fathers*, (Olzog Verlag, Reinelt, 704 pages). He is a revisionist historian considered to be Far Right politically.

a doctor gave me first aid. The road has been asphalted over, but nothing else has been altered.

And people, will they ever change? The two photographs of children playing around the chain cordon before the Arc de Triomphe in Paris seem to answer the question. They are of the same age, and though separated by fifty years in time have the same fascination for the chain. Children grow up to be adults. Thus we know there will always be wars, what we do not know is when, where and how often.

Appendix 1

Field Post Letters to My Mother

The field post was an essential part of the war routine. This small selection of field post letters shows two factors: the agonizing nostalgia for the home province and the constant fear of never returning; and the enduring hope for a quick peace. In my own case, writing and receiving letters were the most important things in life for the soldier at war and the mother at home. The letters show too that the German soldier was not at the front fighting each and every day, nor was he eternally shouting Heil Hitler! but tried to live his life as near normally as possible throughout a war which with the passing of the years became ever more brutal.

3 August 1943

Dear Mother

We are finally back from the training grounds. We went by bicycle since there were no vehicles. It was a fine old puff in the heat, something like seventy kilometres uphill and downhill. Posadowsky went on leave yesterday, he got only fourteen days despite his wife applying for four weeks' farming leave which had been approved and recommended by everyone. Here he got it as convalescence leave. If you have anything to send him then send it to him and he will take it with him: Graf Posadowsky, Klein Peterwitz, Kreis Guhrau, Silesia. His wife has a very good contact, high up in some General Staff or other, and if he sends her a cable "Friedrich very ill" then she has to leave at once, drop everything, head west to her parents at Mainz. Then it would be ready. He just wrote that the state of health is very critical. You will know more but one cannot write everything. If we shall spend much more time here is still uncertain.

30 April 1944

Dear Mother

I have kept going and will soon be in Rumania. I wouldn't mind if we went a bit faster ... and I am filthy again, do you remember the nice clean uniform which I came home. Well, I'm fed up with it. All the time I dream of my next leave or even better to live as a civilian. How it sickens me – dirty hands, black fingernails, face and hair always filthy, and then the tiny visitors move in! Let's hope it's all over soon. I am fed up to here with it. I am still so full of leave and freedom that I still have to pick up where I left off. I look longingly at every hospital train and think how lovely it would be to have a little wound that keeps me in Germany. It is certainly not right to think like that but as time goes on one cannot help it.

Anyway, I'll go down to the unit first to see how things are. The sister regiment, which has been in Russia since the first day, has now been transferred out to France with its division. Perhaps there will be an invasion in June, that's how things are looking. Will find out if the comrades have got new vehicles. Fate was kind to me again by letting me see Vienna for four days. If everything with the leave trains had gone as it was supposed to, I would already be back with my unit. Anyway, I shall write when I get there. By the way I took the wrong scissors, I wanted a pair with a bent cutting surface.

Therefore when I remember my leave I have to think how I had this unique opportunity to stretch it out and was such an idiot, but one is too honest. At the same time I got three days extra. They were wonderful days. The best were the first days skiing, birthday and Easter, with them I could always say I had another fourteen days' leave, what a long time still. And then the days went by faster. I wonder if I shall have to wait another fourteen months for the next one. You don't believe so, I know, but what do dreams count. The worst of it is that I am in a cattle truck amongst thick peasants (the worst society makes you feel that you are a person amongst people) am travelling through and to a country where there are many things wrong. One should not lose belief in the return to the good old times even if it will never be the same as it was.

14 May 1944
Dear Mother

Back with my unit, naturally back in a panzer. The squadron has had an idyllic rest for some time in an orchard. The prints will be ready now. I have heard there is a ban on packets. If you have not sent them yet, keep them and I'll have a leave-taker collect them. Now is naturally open-season for leave and there is a lot of coming and going. So, I do not have this worry any more. It is only right that I should get some more soon. Air mail stamps enclosed.

I wrote on the envelope of letter 9 that I lost my baggage again. Duplicity! The wagon carrying it could not cross the Dniestr because the bridges were down. So it stayed where it was and so either the Russians have it or it has floated down the Dniestr to the Black Sea. With it have gone my best brushes. Yesterday I boiled my black shirt, when wringing it out I tore it, but that is not so bad. I am only glad to have taken my change of clothing with me, and so I only lost one pair of pants. There is much else lost, especially such essential things as cooking utensils and field flask. I shall finish here for today.

Zinten, 27 January 1945
My dear Mother

The situation is getting worse daily, the circle is closing. Today the Wehrmacht bulletin reported street fighting in Elbing, which means we are encircled on land and in Zinten I am at the centre of it. 24.Pzr.Div. is deployed here, which is the only consolation, if I had been KV'd earlier I would have been with them in the encirclement. I have been lucky so far, everyone was rooted out except the cripples and amputees. Even more luck, the whole unit has been sent to the front, only the cripples and amputees remain behind. Recently there was a Seven to winkle out the lesser wounded, if that happens again they will net me. Then we shall have to defend the barracks, but nobody knows from which direction Ivan will come. There is still a high Staff here which is a small consolation, for where these people set up with their *Blitzfrauen* [female signals staff: Tr.] they are always well back behind the lines – but will I get out of this encirclement?

I don't know if this letter will arrive. Who knows what horrors are still to come and if we shall ever meet again. I have just gone through my photos, I had a wonderful childhood and am very grateful to you for it. What wonderful days they were on the Feldberg or Schauinsland, skiing or playing tennis. That was simply wonderful. There were even some good days with the military, at the Army Ski Championship on the Feldberg or in Sagan on the tennis courts, in beautiful Naples or blessed Normandy, Rouen, Lisieux, Paris, Pisa, Livorno, Viareggio were not so bad.

So now we sit here, waiting with our bags packed to run for it. And if you stick your nose outside for five minutes, you get the feeling we are ready to up and be off. The fare is now excellent, meat, butter, schnapps, chocolate, but that is always a bad sign. For you these hours and days will be very difficult, I am still young and we recover from these things easier. Many corporals and sergeants have their wives and children here. Some were on the way to the West but the coaches had to stop or turn back at Elbing. Here the window panes are trembling, the artillery fire is very near and goes on all day. Early on Sunday I was in Allenstein by the way, it was still very quiet and in the evening the Russians captured it. Apparently with seven tanks! I hope you get this letter. I shall close here.

Heiligenbeil, 6 February 1945

Dear Mother

The AV-people [cripples] are now leaving for Germany. And I have to go before the doctor again, they will probably declare me KV and I shall have to go to the front. The worst is that we shall have to fight as infantry. Well, I'll probably come through OK.

Neuruppin, 20 February 1945

On the journey here I used every opportunity to write letters, despite that I believe it must take a long time until the mail gets to you. It if arrives at all. Mail from Heiligenbeil goes airmail to Berlin but the Berlin people have not received it. I will tell you a little about my journey. On 1 February we drove to Heiligenbeil and awaited events. After six days we all had a medical examination to see if we were fit for the front. I told them I had burns, heart problem and difficulty in seeing. After the stethoscope probably the heart was decisive and they wrote me up unfit for the front. I ought to add there was an examination in Zinten previously, I had guard duty and – I really cannot explain why I forgot to include this – the examination passed me by. On the 7th we began our difficult move to Leisunnen Haff. The baggage went on a wagon to that point.

We had to walk and then we tramped over the ice, constantly up to our ankles. After seven kilometres on the ice I was wet to above the knees, it was raining torrentially and I had to wear the heavy backpack. There were a couple of plundered clothing items. Pity I cannot send a parcel any more. In the meantime I lost my gas mask case in the water. It took four days from Heiligenbeil to Danzig. Went along the entire Nehrung, only rode a bit at the end. That was about 100 kilometres, a laudable feat with my heavy backpack. Amongst thousands of refugees and carts. What the East Prussian people have gone through is indescribable and without parallel. Women gave premature birth on the ice, old people dead by the wayside, often seven or eight carts would go under when the ice gave way.

When we got to Danzig that was the worst bit behind us, now I had to escape the second encirclement. After a wait of four days we went by goods waggon attached to a hospital train and so came to Neuruppin. It is not certain if we shall stay here. Let's hope we from Zinten have another unit for us, it is not very nice here. KV, doctor, etc. Nothing better will be available, the courier time as at Zinten is over. Fingers crossed we shan't have to see the doctor. There are still so many stumbling blocks to be overcome. Tomorrow I could be at the front, and then one has no idea what will happen.

Appendix 2

Essays at High School, 1939–1940

Two German essays written by the pupils of form 7c at the Berthold Gynmnasium, Freiburg im Breisgau, in the school year 1939/1940. These essays show the influence of the Nazi State: they might almost have come from the pen of Propaganda Minister Goebbels.

Berthold Gymnasium, Class Essay 26 May 1939.

Air Raid Precautions (ARP) at our House.

Introduction
1. ARP as a new method.
2. Air Raid courses for the entire population
3. What are the serious dangers from the air?

Main Part
a. Clearing out junk.
b. Blacking-out.
c. Setting up the protected room.
d. ARP in large factories and concerns.

Conclusion
ARP is self protection!

When we talk today of ARP, this term is a matter of routine. A few years ago it did not exist for us, and we did not know how important it would be for the whole population. Even in the Great War there was no ARP in the modern sense, it was known only to the military. Some inhabitants did black-out now and again, but on the whole no measures were taken to protect the people. During an attack by aircraft one fled to a cellar, sometimes a really inadequate refuge was found. Not until now has a planned education for the people been introduced. All danger points have been considered down to the smallest detail and all important questions thought through and resolved. Today everybody knows that in the event of an air raid he has to go to the shelter appointed. Everybody has his appointed post which he must administer conscientiously and with circumspection.

What are the dangers which threaten us from the air? First there are HE bombs: splinter bombs, explosive bombs and land mines. For residential areas the latter will be a rarity because they are costly to manufacture and the enemy will prefer to use them against important installations such as railway stations, bridges and public utilities. If a person lives near such places he has to take into account the possibility that his house will be hit by one or destroyed by the blast and air pressure from nearby. Our main interest lies in incendiaries and poison gas-bombs.

Incendiaries are very dangerous especially because they are very light and an aircraft can carry many of them. These bombs lodge in the roof of a house and start a fire there. It is the job of the fire brigade to extinguish such fires with the means at their disposal. Gas masks protect against gas bombs. Everybody must obtain a practical mask. A rubber hood can be drawn very close to the head, and a large filter allows easy breathing.

ARP as an Innovation

A. The term ARP applied to a house does not mean the cellar exclusively. The alarm preparedness begins with the roof. Lofts filled to the rooftops with junk must be cleared out! Already lofts are being cleared and equipped thinking of ARP. Treated beams and floors protect against fire and a layer of sand prevents fire penetrating through to the lower floor and can even be effective against bombs. If possible every storey should have a fire hydrant, sandbox and hose, but most important of all many water containers. If a fire develops, every occupant of a house must know how to put it out with the means available. This may prevent a fire spreading.

B. The first duty of the house occupants is to black-out the windows (the black-out arrangements must be adequate for the windows: blacking-out window frames with no glass is difficult work). Blacking-out should be possible with just a few hand movements, and the materials must always be stored in a convenient place. During black-out blue light bulbs are best. There are also black-out pasteboard covers for lamps but there are not very practical since they catch fire easily. I would always carry a pocket torch which is very good covered by a handkerchief.

C. Equipping the air raid shelter, which must offer protection to all occupants and neighbours, requires the greatest attention to detail. Above all it must be resistant to collapse and gas. It must have seating for everybody, enough space for people to lie down, warm blankets and coats (which are usually forgotten in the haste to get down there). The ARP medical box is very important. It should contain sterile bandages, gauze and cotton wadding, also tranquillizers, vaseline or boric acid ointment and several triangular cloths. This box should already have been prepared.

In the event of war it is essential to keep sealed boxes of food ready to eat and above all fresh drinking water. Books to shorten long hours of waiting and toys for children are very desirable (supplied here are only the most necessary measures in outline: in case of necessity it is the duty of the lady of the house to complete the ARP shelter as best she can). It must always be remembered that many people will be in these shelters for hours or days and there will be a certain snugness. Too much, or too loud conversation and movement is to be avoided since this will use up much oxygen. Air is precious! It should be obvious that no flame should be exposed nor should anybody smoke. The entrance to the shelter may become blocked by debris, therefore a pickaxe, shovel and other tools should be on hand for clearing such obstructions. I would indicate clearly cupboards and cases in which protective suits, gas masks, steel helmets etc are kept so that strangers to the shelter can see them at once and avoid unnecessary searching.

D. The shelter must also be completely gasproof. In a self-contained house the preparations for air raid drill are relatively easy to carry out as opposed to the difficulties of the organisational technicques in a large concern, factory, school or hospital. Arrows should point the way to the air raid shelter. The way there should be clearly marked. It is especially difficult in factories, where flammable explosive mateials are being worked upon, to provide adequate protection against any danger of fire.

Conclusion: Educating an entire nation in ARP awareness is a major task which above all requires groundwork. There are still people today who doubt the need for ARP, but even in the last war it was seen that if properly blacked-out a locality is almost impossible to find. ARP requires that in wartime the house will always be ready to deal with an alarm. ARP affords protection not only in war, it will also protect agaainst damage in peacetime too. Courage and skill are our best self-defence.

Observation: The teacher criticized the failure to mention a responsible demeanour in ARP.

House Essay, 13 March 1940.
Which Mental and Material Strengths does the War require of us?
Today, twenty-five years after the Great War, those same enemy forces have arisen to encircle and fragment Germany. Our opponents are the same as

those of 1914. The old forces of Versailles are still alive and are resolved to the uttermost to take up the threads of their old policies.

Our enemies have found common ground in the most diverse motives: this one envious of our trade, the other wanting parts of our territory, but all probably sniff a great chance of financial gain. Thus Germany is forced to prevent a repeat of our misfortune, and the 1914 and 1939 generations stand together, weapons in hand, determined to defend their right of existence to final victory. Thus we are in the midst of war. Mindful of his duty the German soldier fulfils his mission at the front. In the West he is protected by a defensive wall unequalled in world history. It is not difficult to make the German familiar with his duty for the military qualities are in his blood.

In today's State every man is a soldier. Just as the man in field-grey fulfils his duty at the front, so there is an internal front which has to be stretched to the uttermost of its capabilities and knowledge in the service of the Fatherland. Weaving and interlacing work into a totality is the great business of the times. Britain knows well that National Socialist Germany, the best military State in the world, cannot be got the better of by military means. Therefore she is trying to defeat us by an economic blockade and starvation. As a defence, to farming falls the foremost task, to feed the German people by German work on German soil. A special effort must be made to increase the productivity of the land and so raise it to a level to cover requirements. Thus it falls to farming to secure our needs in foodstuffs. All available means must be used for this purpose.

Because the farmer will usually be conscripted, his wife may have to run the farm alone. That is an extraordinary burden for a woman but provisions have been made for it. The female RAD workforce and above all the Hitler Youth have become a great help by appropriate involvement.

As the second important factor we have industry. Here the armaments industry must have priority. Clearly not even the best State can resist with inadequate weapons. The munitions factories are working night and day. German engineers have designed the fastest and most reliable aircraft. Numerous U-boats continue to flow off the production lines, also guns of all kinds. The German people have not only the best but also the best-armed soldiers. Although we know that armaments work is surrounded by great difficulties, the term "impossible" belongs in the past!

Enormous activity is now entering the war, and the search is on for the last reserves of the workforce. We know that a great amount of raw materials especially important for the armaments industry like cotton, rubber, copper and other materials cannot be obtained in sufficient quantities from German soil. We also know that the German spirit of inventiveness in the past has succeeded in resolving the most difficult problems. The inventive skill of technologists and chemists has discovered possibilities and weapons freeing industry of reliance on vital imports from abroad.

The German people must assist by saving valuable raw materials, handing in above all old iron, empty tubes, jute sacks and similar items which have no value for the individual and so provide valuable help for the nation as a whole.

In the *Kriegswinterhilfswerk* [war-winter national charity] everybody should prove his solidarity with the whole nation by contributing as much as he can. It must be the natural duty of every German to save. Today all excess money belongs in the savings bank in order to be useful to the Fatherland. Equally important in war is education: never should the highest good of the nation, those who carry the genotype from the past into the future, nor the education of youth itself, be neglected.

Every man must do his duty as in peacetime. Newspapers, literature and above all radio form parts of the field of education. They are the mental nourishment of the adult, they control daily, almost hourly, the opinions and thoughts of all members of the Volk. They form and give shape to the picture which enables every individual to relate his near and distant environments to the total events on this Earth. These weapons of extraordinary significance must never be influenced by foreigners. It has long been known that the Western Powers hold out great hopes in their radio propaganda. Their listeners here, first softened up by "facts", are now being bombarded with false information which has certainly been partially successful in its aim and purpose of creating confusion and subversion and sowing mistrust. Therefore the ban on listening to foreign radio broadcasts is well-founded and forward-looking. Everybody must understand that every day the weapons of subversion and influence are being aimed at him. This involves the civilian in the defensive struggle, for the attack through the ether is just another form of warfare. Foreign nationals did not reckon with the obedience of the German people, and so these "air attacks" on Germany failed not only for the law banning listening to them, but through the caution of every individual listener!

The German Volk is now involved in its decisive struggle for existence and has embarked upon the decisive year of history. If every individual carries out his duty to the best of his ability as a link in the great chain, so the nation, united inwardly and mighty outwardly, will be the eternally free Homeland of all Germans. It is our desire that nobody shall rob us of victory and that our youth shall prove itself on the battlefield, determined to preserve what men before us have won spiritually and in reality.

The tutor found the content of this essay reasonably good and on 17 March 1940 awarded it three out of five.

Bibliography

Bacque, J., *Der geplante Tod. Deutsche Kriegsgefangene in amerikanischen und französischen Lagern 1945 – 1946* (Frankfurt a.M. – Berlin 1993).

Bamm, P., *Eines Menschen Zeit* (Zurich 1972).

Bartov, O., *Hitlers Wehrmacht* (Hamburg 1995).

Bauer, E., *Der Panzerkrieg*, Band 2 (Bonn 1965).

Benn, G., *Briefe an Ellinor Büller, 1930 – 1937* (Stuttgart 1992).

Benz, W., *Zwischen Hitler und Adenauer* (Frankfurt a.M. 1991).

Berliner Lokalanzeiger, 19.02.1943.

Boberrach, H., *Jugend unter Hitler* (Düsseldorf 1982).

Böttger, A., *Mit der Kamera dabei*, KIT 2/90.

Böttger, A. und Heitzer, Th., 'Die Uniformen mit der goldgeben Waffenfarbe', *Internationales Militaria-Magazin* (September 2001).

Dahms, H. G., *Der 2. Weltkrieg* (München – Berlin 1989).

Der springende Reiter (Hannover 1994).

Der springende Reiter (Hannover 1996).

Faller, H., *Frankfurter Allgemeine Zeitung*, 30.09.1991.

Fest, J. C., *Hitler* (Frankfurt a.M., Berlin, Wien 1973).

Filbinger, H., *Die geschmähte Generation* (München 1987).

Fraschka, G., *Mit Schwertern und Brillanten* (München 1994).

Goethe, J. W., *Campagne in Frankreich* (Frankfurt a.M. und Leipzig 1994).

Götz, H. H., *Frankfurter Allgemeine Zeitung*, 9.09.1991.

Hauschild, R., *Der springende Reiter* (Gross-Umstadt 1984).

Hauschild, R., *Flammendes Haff* (München 1986).

Hinze, R., *Rückzugskämpfe in der Ukraine 1943/44* (Meerbusch 1991).

Hinze, R., *Mit dem Mut der Verzweiflung* (Meerbusch 1993).

Hochhuth, R., *Ein Leibe in Deutschland* (Hamburg 1978).

Jodl, L., *Jenseits des Endes* (München – Wien 1987).

Keitel, W., *Erinnerungen, Briefe, Dokumente des Chefs des Oberkommandos der Wehrmacht* (Schnellbach 1998).

Kershaw, I., *Hitler* (Stuttgart 1998).

Klüger, R., *Weiter leben* (Göttingen 1993).

Koschorrek, G., *Vergiss die Zeit der Dornen nicht* (Mainz 1998).

Kraus, O./Kulka, E., *Die Todesfabrik* (Berlin 1991).

Lehmann, R., *Die Leibstandarte*, Band 3 (Osnabrück 1982).

Magenheimer, H., *Abwehrschlacht an der Weischel 1945* (Freiburg i.Br. 1986).

Maser, W., *Friedrich Ebert* (Frankfurt a.M. – Berlin 1990).

Naumann, G., *Lauscher bei Florian* (Leoni am Starnberger See 1993).

Niederschlesische Allgemeine Volkszeitung (Sagner Wochenblatt) 15.02.1942.

Oberkommando der Wehrmacht, *Soldatenbriefe zur Berufsförderung*, 1942.

Oberkommando der Wehrmacht, *Tornisterschrift*, 1942.

Page, H. P., *General Friedrich Olbricht* (Bonn – Berlin 1992).

Poeppel, H./Prinz von Preussen, W. K./v. Hase, K. G. (Hrsg.), *Die Soldaten der Wehrmacht* (München 1998).

Proske, R., *Wider den Missbrauch der Geschichte deutscher Soldtaen zur politischen Zwecken* (Mainz 1996).

Przybylski, P., *Täter neben Hitler* (Wiesbaden 1990).

Rinke, H., *Unser Regiment im Bild* (Gross-Umstadt 1990).

Ritter, G., *Carl Goerdeler und die deutsche Widerstandsbewegung* (Stuttgart 1984).

Schadewaldt, H., *Von der Medizinischen Akademie zur Universität* Düsseldorf, Festschrift (Berlin 1973).

Scheurig, B., *Alfred Jodl* (Berlin, Frankfurt a.M. 1991).

v. Senger und Etterlin, F. M., *Die 24. Panzerdivision* (Friedberg/H. 1986).

Stahlberg, A., *Die verdammte Pflicht* (Frankfurt a.M., Berlin 1990).

Sturm und Drang, Nr. 4 (Tokio 1992).

Vollnhals, C., *Entnazifizierung* (München 1991).

Warlimont, W., *Im Hauptquartier der Deutsche Wehrmacht 1939-1945*, Band 1 und 2 (Augsburg 1990).

Weidemann, G.-A., *Unser Regiment* (Gross-Umstadt 1984).

Wette, W., 'Die Legende von der sauberen Wehrmacht', *Frankfurter Allgemeine Zeitung* 6.04.1995.

Williamson, G., *Die SS* (Klagenfurt 1998).

Winters, J. P., *Frankfurter Allgemeine Zeitung* 5.10.1991.